Microsoft®, Word®, Excel®, Outlook®, and PowerPoint® are registered trademarks of Microsoft Corporation.

Conventions used:

Keys to be pressed are enclosed in parenthesis such as: press (Enter).

Text to be typed, when included in an exercise step will be shaded, for example:
Type *No Fault Travel* and then press (Enter).

Be sure to check out our website: www.LutherMaddy.com to contact the author, order these books in quantity, or see other resources available for this workbook.

Table of Contents

Lesson #1: Creating and Saving Documents 2
  The Word Window 2
  Saving Documents.. 4
  The Save As dialog box 6
    Save vs. Save As 7
  Modifying the Status Bar display 7
  Changing Views... 9
    Zoom Settings 10
  Print Preview: 11
  Printing Documents 12
  Closing a Document: 13
  Lesson #1: Skill Builder 14
  Check Yourself 15
Lesson #2: Basic Editing 18
  Opening Files 18
  Moving the Insertion Point 19
  Delete Existing Text with the Keyboard 19
  Auto Spell Check 21
  Saving an Existing Document 22
  Lesson #2: Skill Builder 23
  Check Yourself 24
Lesson #3 – Using The Help Task Pane 26
  Help 26
  Lesson #3: Skill Builder 28
  Check Yourself 28
Lesson #4: Selecting, Moving, Copying, and Enhancing text 30
  Selecting Text... 30
  Moving (Cutting) and Copying text.. 31
  The Paste Options Smart Tag 33
  Using the Undo Command 33
  Using the Shortcut Menu to Move and Copy 34
  Using Drag and Drop to Move and Copy 35
  Enhancing Existing Text 37
  Using the Format Painter 41
  Using the Mini-Toolbar to Enhance Text... 42
  Using Keyboard Shortcuts to Enhance Text. 43
  Using Save As instead of Save 44
  Enhancing New Text... 45
  Removing Enhancements.. 48
  The Clear Formatting Option 49
  Skill Builder Lesson #4 51
  Check Yourself 52
Lesson #5: Basic Paragraph and Page Formatting 54
  Page Setup 54
  Paragraph Formatting... 58

Spacing Between Paragraphs 59
Indenting Paragraphs 61
Hanging Indents... 62
Setting Tabs 64
Table of Contents 65
Using the Ruler to Set Tabs... 65
Using Tab Leaders... 67
Adjusting Tabs with the Ruler Bar.. 69
Skill Builder: Lesson #5 71
Check Yourself 72

Lesson #6: Envelopes and Labels..**74**
Creating Envelopes 74
Creating Labels.. 76
Skill Builder: Lesson #6 82
Check Yourself 82

Lesson #7: Find and Replace...**84**
Finding Text 84
Replacing Text.. 84
Using the Thesaurus... 86
Skill Builder: Lesson #7 87
Check Yourself 87

Lesson #8: Creating and Formatting Tables.......................................**88**
Merging cells 88
Inserting rows in a table... 90
Splitting Table Cells... 91
Changing Text Direction 93
Table Cell Alignment.. 93
Formatting the Table.. 95
Table Formulas 96
Using the Table Styles.. 98
Changing Column Widths 99
Skill Builder: Lesson #7 102

Microsoft Word Shortcut Keys..**103**

Welcome to Word 2010 Basics

This series of workbook/reference manuals are designed to get you working more productively with MS Word. You may be using this book on your own or in class. Either way, this module will focus on the basics; the things every Word user should know to use Word to the fullest. In addition to learning basic Word features, you'll begin to learn more about using it more productively.

The difference between simply using Word and using it for utmost productivity can be huge. I encourage you to spend some time going over the topics covered in this module, even if you've been using Word for quite a while. Invariably, there will be some things you'll learn that will make you a better, more productive user.

This workbook is meant to be used in its entirety. Lessons build on the files created in previous lessons. This means you'll need to start at the beginning and work through each lesson in order for the later lessons to work correctly. If you're already familiar with the concepts taught in the early lessons, go ahead and complete them anyway. You're existing skills will enable you to complete them very quickly. And, who knows, you may even learn a thing or two in those lessons as well.

Luther M. Maddy IIII, Ph.D.

 6/14

Lesson #1: Creating and Saving Documents

In this lesson you will learn to:

Create Documents
Save Documents
Modifying the Status bar display
Change the View
Use the Print Preview feature

© 2011 Luther M. Maddy III

Lesson #1: Creating and Saving Documents

The Word Window

1. Start Word if needed.

You can start Word several ways. If you do not have a desktop icon, use the Windows start button to locate MS Word.

When you first open Word you'll see what essentially equates to a blank piece of paper. You should see a blinking vertical bar which is called the insertion point. The insertion point is where any text you type will appear. The insertion point shows you what text will be erased or changed if you are editing.

Obviously there is a little more showing up here than a piece of blank paper so take a few minutes and examine the Word window, the illustration below and the descriptions for the items listed in this manual.

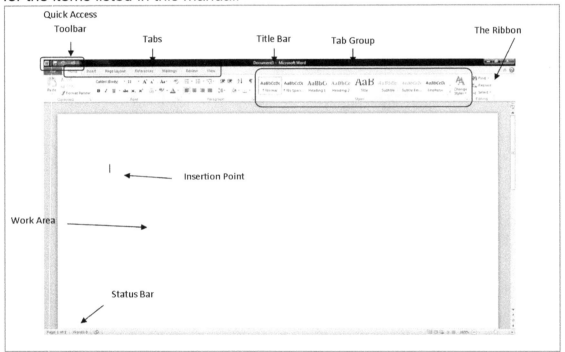

The Title Bar: Identifies the program you are working in and will display the name of the document you are working on. A new document will not have a name until you save it for the first time.

The Ribbon: The Ribbon gives you quick access to the feature you are working on. You can display different commands by clicking the Tabs above the ribbon. The ribbon will change, depending on what features you are working within Word.

The Quick Access toolbar: Provides a quick way to access commonly used commands, like saving a document, or undoing your last action.

         6/14

The Status Bar: The Status Bar keeps you informed as to which page you are on and where on that page the insertion point is.

The Work area: This is where you will type or edit the document.

2.   **In an empty Word document window, type the following, ensuring that you press (Enter) only at the end of each paragraph.**

> MS Word is a very powerful word processing program. With it, you can easily create and format your documents. You can also easily perform tasks that were once very complex such as envelopes, labels and forms.
>
> As you learn more about MS Word, you will come to appreciate its power and ease of use. Just remember that learning any new program takes time. Just be patient and you will soon be creating documents like a professional word processor.

The above text that you are typing is shaded because that is how this text will identify text you are to type. You will not need to shade the text you are typing unless specifically instructed to in this text.

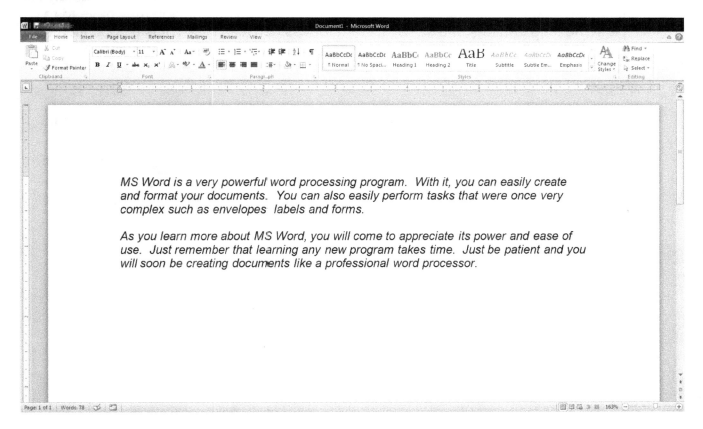

© 2011 Luther M. Maddy III

You can create the blank line between these two paragraphs by pressing (Enter) twice after the first paragraph. Your default (automatic) settings may cause Word to add the blank line between paragraphs automatically. We'll cover this later in this book.

 Question: When is a paragraph not a paragraph?
Answer: When you do not complete it by pressing the "Enter" key!

Your screen may not look exactly like the illustration depending on the view you have selected. We'll discuss view settings in the next couple of pages. The blank areas around the text in the illustration are the margins.

Saving Documents

If you do not want to lose everything you have typed, you will need to save the Word document. Currently this document is stored in your computer's RAM (Random Access Memory). When you lose power or turn off your computer, everything in RAM is lost. Saving stores the file on a disk, flash drive or cloud storage.

Once saved, you can then retrieve (Open) it again when you need it at a later date. You should develop the habit of saving very frequently. If you do not, you may have to re-type some long portions of text. Since hard drives can also crash, it is a good idea to store important documents in at least two places to ensure against their loss. For example, you can store the novel you are creating on your computer's hard drive and also on a flash (thumb) drive. This way, should one copy be lost, you have the other.

To save a document for the first and subsequent times you select the Save command.

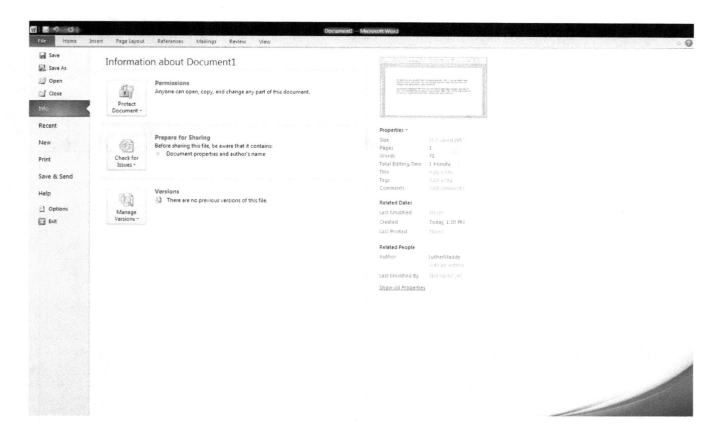

3.   Click the File command and choose Save.
You could also access the Save command from the Quick Access toolbar.

The Save As dialog box

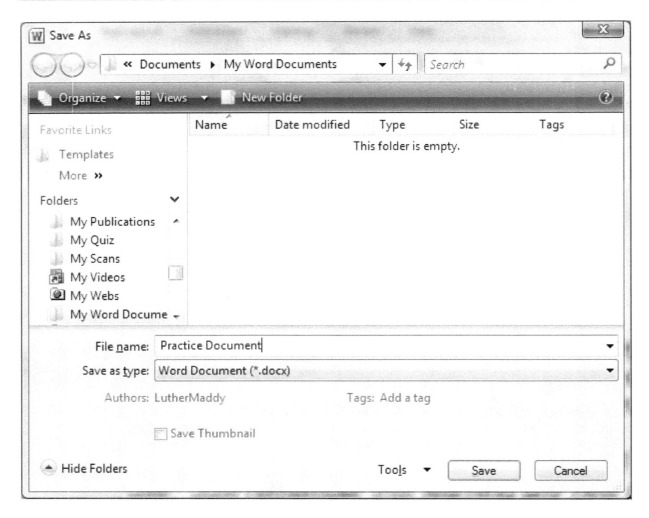

When you choose the Save command for the first time, Word will display the Save As dialog box. This is because you have not yet saved this file and will need to give this file a name. You will use this name to refer to this file when you want to use it again.

In addition to the file name, you can also specify where (which drive) the file should be stored. In most cases you will store your files on your computer's hard drive which is usually designated drive C: or D:.

Before saving, it is a good idea to notice the folder you are placing this file in. This makes locating the file much easier. There are likely many folders on your hard drive and knowing where to look for a file makes finding it much easier.

Your Save As and Open dialog boxes may appear slightly different from those illustrated in this book. The operating system you are using can affect these slightly. While these dialog boxes may differ slightly, the commands are the same regardless of your operating system.

4.   In the File Name text box, type: *Practice document.*

> 👍 *Hint: You do not need to click in the file name text box. When you start typing, Word will erase the existing name.*

Word attempts to choose a file name for you from your document. Filenames can be quite large but when you name a file, you want to give it a name that is short enough to show up in a list but also descriptive so you can find the file again in a large list of files. Officially, filenames can be up to 255 characters in length, but file names of this size are quite unwieldy. You can include spaces, but you should not use punctuation or other symbols in file names.

5.   After typing the file name, click Save to save the file.

Save vs. Save As

You selected the Save command but Word displayed the Save As dialog box. This is because you had not already named this file. As you continue to make modifications to a document, you will want to save often. However, when you do, choose the Save command, not the Save As command. When you choose the Save command, Word will overwrite the previous version of the file with the newest version and use the same name.

If you choose the Save As command Word will ask if you want to replace the existing file with the one you are saving. If you are working on the same document, you will, of course, want to replace the old with the new. Using the Save command eliminates this extra, sometimes confusing question that Word asks.

One purpose of the Save As command is to make a copy of a file with a different name or in a different location for backup purposes. When you choose Save, Word automatically keeps the same name and the same location. Using the Save As command allows you to change the location, name or both. If you do change either of these, you then have two files, either in the same location with two different names or perhaps with the same name but at two different locations or drives.

Modifying the Status Bar display

You can easily modify the status bar to give you details about your document. For example, you may want to know what page of the document you are looking at, or you may want to know exactly where the insertion point (cursor) is on the page. Word allows you to easily customize the status bar to display important information about your document.

6. Right+Click the Word Status Bar.

If you closely examine this shortcut menu that appears, you will see many properties of the document you can display on the status bar. This menu also gives you the current values of these properties if you do not want to permanently display them on the status bar.

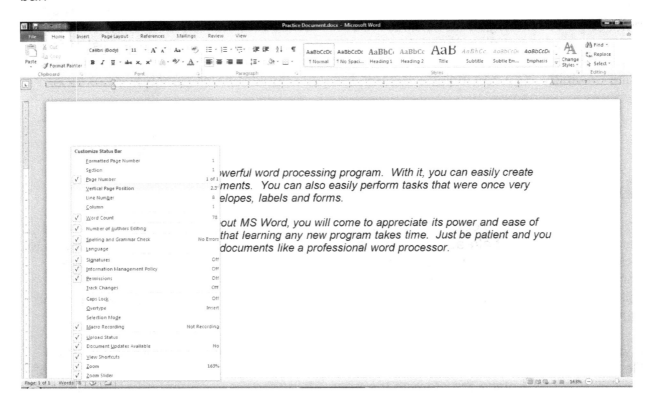

7. From the menu that appears, ensure Vertical Page Position is turned on then click outside the menu.

You should now see the exact vertical position of the insertion point on the page appear on the status bar.

8. Right+Click the status bar again. Turn off Vertical Page Position. Make sure that Page Number, and Word count are turned on.

© 2011 Luther M. Maddy III

Changing Views

Word has several views you can use as you edit and scroll through your document. The two most commonly used are Draft and Print Layout. Of these two, the Print Layout view is usually preferred as it lets you see your document as it will print. You can change the view using the View tab or the View buttons on the right of the status bar. Some of the views available in MS Word are:

Draft View: In this view, not all formatting and other page features will show in this mode.

Print Layout View: This mode shows the document as it will print. Print Layout also displays a vertical ruler and shows the top margin. This is very close to a WYSIWYG (what you see is what you get) editing mode and does show Headers and Footers.

Full Screen Reading: This mode optimizes the view for reading a document on a computer screen. This mode, by default shows two pages side by side and also gives you the option of seeing the document just as it would appear if printed.

You'll now try changing the view of the Word document you just created.

1.   Click the View tab above the ribbon. If the Ruler option is not on, turn it on then click the Draft tool on the Ribbon.

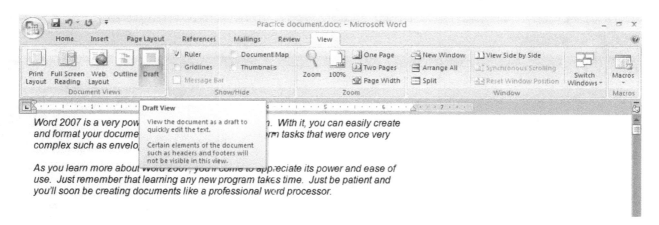

Notice the ruler along the left side of the window is not visible. You may also notice there is no empty space at the top of the page. The draft view does not show the page margins.

2.   Now, click the Print Layout tool on the Ribbon.
The vertical ruler is now visible. This is the view you want to be in most of the time when working in Word.

To change views you can also use the View shortcuts on the Status Bar or use keyboard shortcuts. There is no right or wrong way to switch views or select any other command in MS Word. There is usually more than one way to select Word commands.

Zoom Settings

In addition to changing the view settings, Word also allows you to choose from pre-defined or custom zoom settings. These settings include allowing you to increase the size of the text for editing purposes or shrink the view so you are looking at an entire page. You can access the zoom settings on the View tab.

1. Display the View tab.

You should now see the View ribbon options including the option of toggling the Ruler on and off.

2. Click One Page in the Zoom group on the Ribbon.

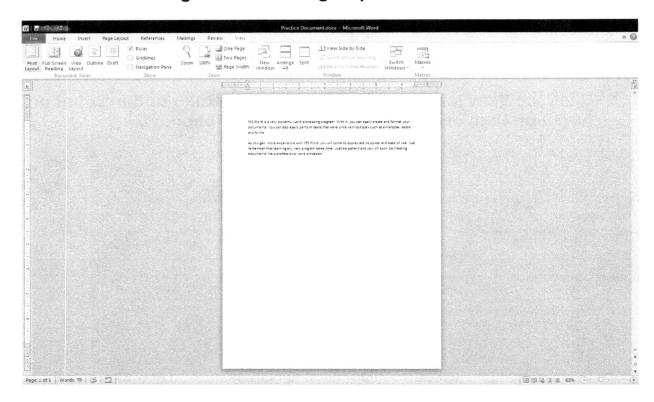

You should now see an entire page of this document. This setting is very useful when you are moving and copying pictures and paragraphs on the same page.

3. Click Page Width in the Zoom group on the Ribbon.

This setting spreads the text out to fill the width of your screen.

4.   Click 100% in the Zoom group on the Ribbon.

This is the normal or default setting in Word.

5.   Choose the view option you prefer, 100% or Page Width.

Many of the screen shots in this text will use the Page Width setting. This allows the text to be more visible in this workbook.

Print Preview:

The only true WYSIWYG mode is the Print Preview mode. Here you see the document exactly as it will print. Clicking anywhere in the print preview screen will zoom into the area where you click.

1.   Click the File menu and then choose Print.

When you click File, Word displays the "Backstage view". This menu allows you to perform many actions. We'll introduce you to some of them in this module.

Word will now display the Print menu which includes a preview of this document.

Printing Documents

The Print menu screen includes several sections and options. Near the top of this screen you will find the Print option. Just to the right of this link you can also select the number of copies you wish to print.

The *Printer* section includes a drop down menu where you can select a printer if you have more than one printer available.

The Printer Properties link just below the printer selected allows you to select printer specific options such as changing the print quality and other options the selected printer may have.

The *Settings* section allows you to specify options such as; duplexing (double sided printing) if your printer has the capability, specific pages to print or paper size and orientation.

To save paper, you don't need to actually print this document.

Closing a Document:

Closing a document allows you to "put it away" and work on something else. As long as you have saved your document after making any changes you will not lose anything. If you have made changes and have not previously saved, Word will warn you to save the document when you attempt to close the document.

2.   Click the Close command on the File menu to close this document.

Lesson #1: Skill Builder

1. **From the File menu click the New option.**

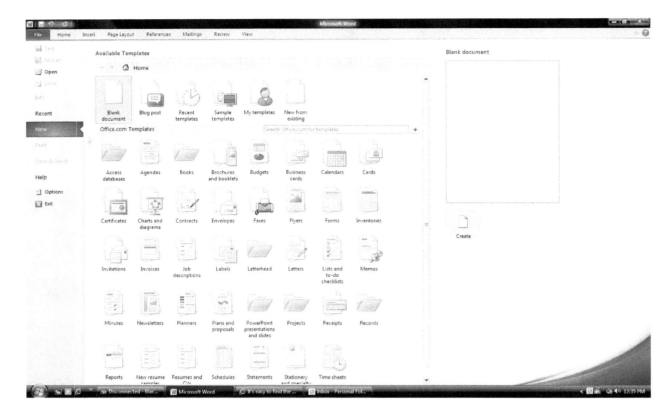

2. **Click the Create button in the right portion of this menu to create a new, blank document.**

3. **Type the following text:**

As requested, we are sending you a list of the current airfares from Boise to Maui. Please be advised that these fares could change at any moment. If you're interested at all, let us know as soon as possible.

Sincerely,

Maria Byrd
Booking Agent

4. **Save this file as *Airfare Request* and close the document.**

Check Yourself

Questions:

1. Where is the Title Bar located?
2. Name two different views available in a Word document?
3. What does Right+Click in the Word Status Bar do?
4. Where is the Zoom tool located?
5. How do you print more than one copy of a document?

Lesson #2: Basic Editing

In this lesson you will learn to:

> *Open Documents*
> *Preview Documents*
> *Move the Insertion point*
> *Delete Existing Text using the Keyboard*
> *Auto Spell Check*
> *Save Existing Document*

Lesson #2: Basic Editing

Opening Files

Once you've closed a document, you'll need to open it if you want to continue working with it. To open a previously saved document you'll use the Open command on the File menu.

1. **Click the File menu option and choose Open to display the Open dialog box.**

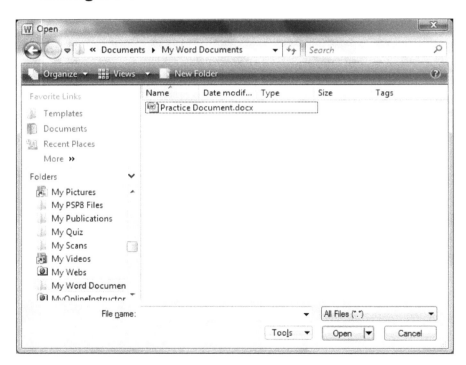

The Open dialog box shows you a list of files in the default (chosen automatically) folder. You can navigate to other folders using this dialog box. You can also use the Views button to see additional information about the files in this folder.

To open a file, just select it by clicking on it and then clicking the Open button at the bottom of this dialog box. You can also open a file by double clicking on it.

2.   In the list of files, click once on *Practice Document* to select it.

The file name will display in a different colored background when it is selected.

3.   Click Open to open this file.

Moving the Insertion Point

The insertion point, sometimes called the cursor, tells you precisely where you are in the text. When you begin typing, the new text will appear at the insertion point's location. The insertion point's location is also very important when editing, adding or deleting text.

You can move the insertion point with the mouse by simply clicking where you want to move the insertion point. You can also move the insertion point using the keyboard. When moving around in a large document, the keyboard is often faster than attempting to use the mouse.

Here are some of the keyboard commands that you can use to move the insertion point within your document:

Move to:	Keystrokes
Top of Document	(Control+Home)
End of Document	(Control+End)
Up one paragraph	(Control+Up Arrow)
Down one paragraph	(Control+Down Arrow)
Beginning of Line	(Home)
End of Line	(End)
Top of Next Page	(Control+Page Down)
Top of Previous Page	(Control+Page Up)
One word right	(Control+Right Arrow)
One word left	(Control+Left Arrow)

Delete Existing Text with the Keyboard

Erase character right of Insertion point	(Delete)
Erase character left of Insertion point	(Backspace)
Erase word left of insertion point	(Control+Backspace)*
Erase word right of insertion point	(Control+Delete)*

Insertion point should be at the beginning of a word

In this portion of Lesson 2 you'll use the keyboard to move the insertion point and edit the text in the Practice document.

1. **After opening the Practice document, press (Control+Down Arrow) until you are at the beginning of the second paragraph.**

When opening a document, Word automatically places the insertion point at the top of the document. (Control+Down Arrow) moves the insertion point down one paragraph each time you press it. If you have a blank line between these two paragraphs, Word considers the blank line a paragraph because you pressed (Enter) to create it.

Whenever you use the Control, Shift or Alt keys, you must keep that key held down while you press the other key.

2. **Press (Control+Right Arrow) twice to move to the beginning of the word** *learn***.**

3. **Press (Control+Delete) to delete this word.**
This deletes the word to the right of the insertion point.

4. **Type the word** *gain* **and press (space) to replace the deleted word.**

5. **Press (Control+Right Arrow) twice again to move to the beginning of *MS Word* in this sentence.**

6. **Press (Control+Backspace) to delete the word** *about*, **the word left of the insertion point.**

7. **Type** *experience with* **and press (space).**

You have replaced the deleted word and your text should appear as that below.

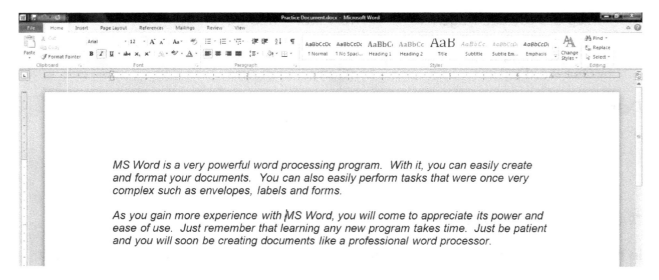

© 2011 Luther M. Maddy III

Auto Spell Check

MS Word automatically checks your spelling and grammar as you type. Word will underline misspelled words, or words not in its dictionary, in red. When it finds a possible grammatical or typographical error, Word will underline the possible error in green.

To quickly correct a word that is underlined in red, move the mouse pointer into that word and right-click. When you do, you will see a list of possible spelling suggestions. If the correct spelling is there, just click it and Word will make the correction for you. If Word underlines words that are spelled correctly, you can select Add from the Spelling shortcut menu to permanently add the word to the spell check dictionary.

1.   **Use the mouse and click inside the word** *"processing"* **in the first line of the first paragraph.**

You can also use the mouse to move the insertion point.

2.   **Now, delete the** *o* **in this word and replace it with an** *e***.**

3.   **Move outside this word and you will see that Word has underlined the word** *precessing* **in red.**

4.   **Move the mouse pointer into this word and right+click.**

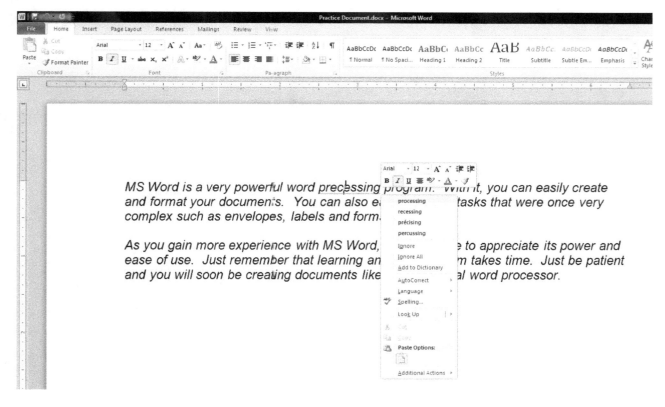

5.   From the list of suggestions, click *processing* **to correct the error.**

Saving an Existing Document

When you save a document that you have already saved, you can choose the Save rather than the Save As command. When you choose Save, Word will save the document with the same name you gave it when you saved it for the first time. This makes the process of saving frequently very easy.

1.   Click the File menu and choose Save.

You may want to try this operation by clicking the Save tool on the Quick Access toolbar. You can also try the keyboard shortcut (Control+S) to save an open document.

When you chose the Save command, Word saved the file as it is right now. The changes you made are saved, and you will not lose them. You will want to develop the habit of regularly saving your document as you work on it. This will ensure that you do not lose any important work.

2.   Click the File menu and choose Close

The document is now closed. Now you must either create a new document or open an existing document.

Lesson #2: Skill Builder

1. **Open the file named *Airfare Request*.**

2. **Using the features covered in lesson #2, make the indicated changes as illustrated below. Delete the text that has a line through it and the text that appears in bold.**

    *As requested, we are ~~sending~~ **enclosing** ~~you~~ a list of the current airfares from Boise to Maui. Please be advised that these fares ~~could~~ **are subject to** change at any moment. ~~If you're interested at all, let~~ **Let** us know as soon as possible **when you're ready to book one of these flights**.*

    Sincerely,

    Maria Byrd
    Booking Agent

When done with this skill builder your text should appear as that below:

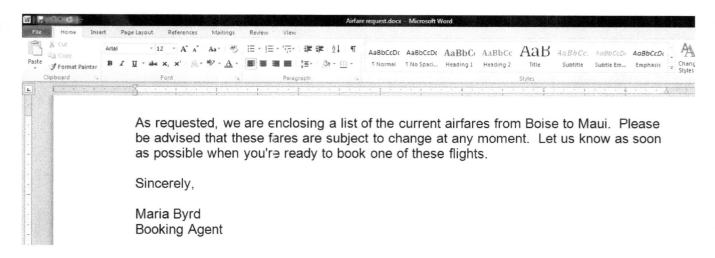

Note: Your lines may break differently than the illustration below depending on the Font and type size you are currently using. You can just ignore that for now. You'll learn to change the font in a later lesson.

3. **Save this file with the same name then Close it.**

Check Yourself

Questions:

1. What is the keyboard command to move to the end of a document.
2. Where does the insertion point move when you press home?
3. How do you move one word to the right?
4. What is an easy way to correct a misspelled word?

Lesson #3: The Help Task Pane

In this lesson you will learn to:

Use Word's Help Feature

Lesson #3 – Using The Help Task Pane

Help

In this lesson we will show you how to use Word's Help feature. Word's help feature has an excellent search feature. To find out how to perform a specific task in Word you can type that task into the search text area and then click Search. Word will often allow you to view specific instructions and even tutorials from some topics.

1.   Open Practice document and press F1 to display the Word Help dialog box.

2.   Type *Save a document*, **in the search text box then click Search.**

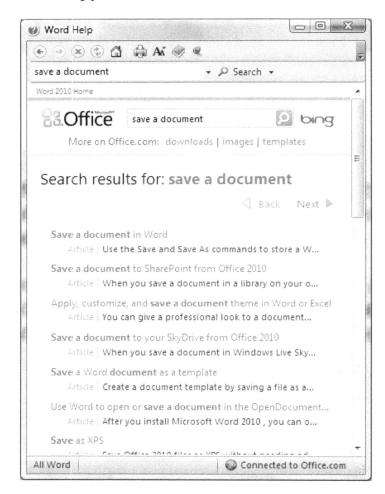

3.   Click on the *Save a document in Word* link in the Help dialog box.

Word now displays a Help window containing links you can click on to access information about the topic.

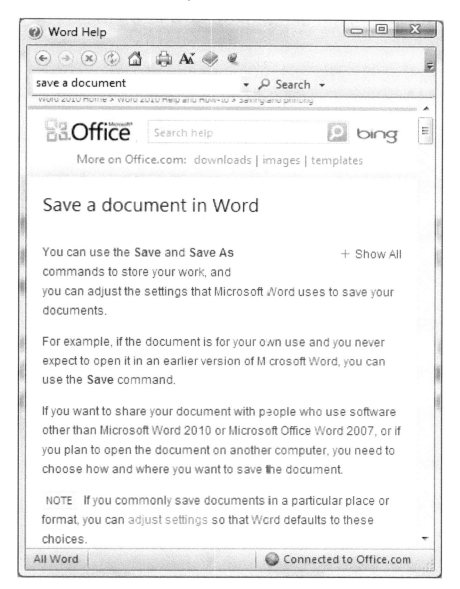

4.   Close the Word help window.

Lesson #3: Skill Builder

1.   Use the Word's help command and lookup how to do the following:

Change the Default Font
> *The default font is the font Word automatically uses when you begin a new document.*

Change the font color

Check Yourself

Questions:

1. What key do you press to display the Word Help dialog box?

Lesson #4: Selecting, Moving, Copying and Enhancing

In this lesson you will learn to:

Select Text with Mouse and Keyboard
Cut, Copy and Paste Text
Drag and Drop Text
Use the Undo Command
Enhance Existing Text
Enhance New Text

Lesson #4: Selecting, Moving, Copying, and Enhancing text

Selecting Text

To change the appearance of existing text or move or copy text you must first select it. Selected text will appear with a blue background and selecting is sometimes called highlighting text. Highlighting is actually a different command so we'll keep calling it Selecting text.

You can select text using the keyboard or the mouse. One very simple way to select text is to simply click and drag across it. However, when you want to select large portions of text this method becomes impractical so here are some other methods you can use to select text.

Selecting text with the mouse within text
Select irregular text portions   Click and drag

You can also position the insertion point at the beginning of the text you want to select and then move the mouse pointer to the end of the text you want to select. To finish the process hold the (Shift) key and click. The text should be selected from where the insertion point was located to where the mouse pointer was located when you clicked with the Shift key held down.

Text to Select	Method with the mouse
Select One Word	Double Click on that word
Select One Paragraph	Triple Click in that paragraph
Select One Sentence	Press (Control) and click in that sentence
Select a Column	Press and hold the (Alt) and drag

Using the Selection area (left margin) and the mouse
The selection area is the left margin, outside of the actual text. When the mouse point is in the selection area it will become an arrow rather than an I-beam.

Text to Select	Selection area method
Select One Line	Click in the selection area to the left of the line
Select One Paragraph	Double click to the left of the paragraph
Select the Entire Document	Triple click in the selection area

Using the keyboard
Text to Select	Keyboard Method
Select One Paragraph	Move to the beginning of the paragraph then (Shift+Control+Down).
Select to End of Document	Move to beginning of desired text, (Shift+Control+End)
Select Entire Document	(Control+A)

Selecting Non-Contiguous Text

Sometimes you may want to select portions of your document that are in different areas (non-contiguous). To do this first select the first portion of text, then hold the Control key and select the other portion of text. This is useful when you want to enhance (bold, underline, etc..) multiple portions of your document.

Moving (Cutting) and Copying text

To move (cut) or copy text you can
      a. Select the text you want to move
      b. Choose Cut or Copy
      c. Move the insertion point where you want the text to be
      d. Choose Paste

What can make this process confusing is that you can choose the Cut, Copy, and Paste commands so many different ways. You can find these commands in the Clipboard group on the Home ribbon, or you can access them with Shortcut keys. This lesson will give you an idea of the variety available with these commands.

You will now open the document you just created and move and copy portions of the text. You will also change the appearance of existing text by selecting that text and making the desired format changes. We'll now have you practice the features we've been discussing here.

1.   Open Practice document.

2.   Move the mouse pointer into the text of the first paragraph and click three times to select the entire paragraph.

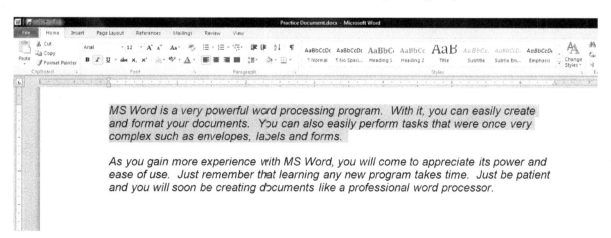

If you're unable to select the text by triple-clicking, make sure you hold the mouse still while you click. The blue highlighting tells you the text is selected.

3.   With this paragraph selected, click the Cut (scissors) tool on the Ribbon.

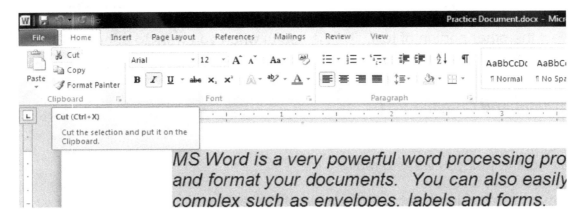

The paragraph you selected will now disappear. The paragraph is not gone forever, it is being stored in the Windows clipboard. You will now move the insertion point where you want the paragraph to be moved and Paste it from the clipboard.

4.   Move the insertion point below the second paragraph with (Control+End).

If you cannot get the insertion point below the paragraph, you neglected to press (Enter) at the end of the second paragraph when creating this document. To correct this, just press the (Enter) now to end the second paragraph. If the insertion point did move below the second paragraph, you do not need to press (Enter).

5.   After moving the insertion point, click the Paste (clipboard) tool on the Ribbon.

The Paste Options Smart Tag

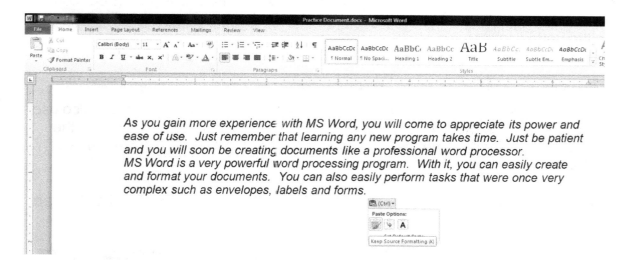

The paragraph that was at the top of the document originally should now be moved below what was the second paragraph.

You may also notice an icon appears at the bottom of the paragraph you just moved. This is a smart tag. Smart tags give you additional options after you perform certain commands.

Clicking on the drop-down arrow of a smart tag or pressing the (Control) key reveals the options available from that tag. This smart tag allows you to choose options that deal with the formatting of the pasted paragraph. Since this document has no additional formatting at the moment, we'll ignore this smart tag.

Using the Undo Command

Whenever you are not happy with the results of a change you just made, you can use the undo command to reverse that change. You can undo several times, however; be careful not to go too far backwards or you may end up undoing something you meant to keep.

You can find the Undo command on the Quick Access toolbar. You can also use the shortcut key (Control+Z).

6. Click the Undo tool on the Quick Access Toolbar twice to undo the move of the first paragraph.

You can undo several times, correcting a series of mistakes. However, be aware that Word will also undo "good" actions like typing text. Be very careful if you un-do more than one or two operations at once. If you undo too far back, you can use the Redo tool to undo the undo command.

Using the Shortcut Menu to Move and Copy

If you use the mouse to select the text you intend to move or copy, you should also use the mouse to select the move or copy commands. The most efficient way to use the mouse is to employ shortcut menus. Using Word's shortcut menus, you can quickly choose the commands you need.

1.   **If needed, select the top paragraph in this document (click three times).**

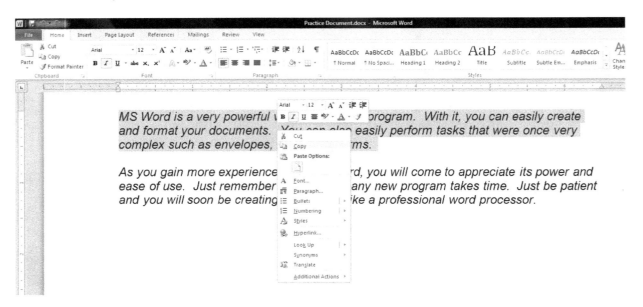

2.   **Move the mouse pointer into the selected paragraph and right+click until you see the menu shown above.**

3.   **From the shortcut menu, click Copy.**

4.   **Now, move the mouse pointer below the second paragraph and right+click.**
     If you cannot get below the last paragraph you need to press (Enter) to create a blank line.

5.   From this shortcut menu, click the first icon, Keep Source Formatting in the Paste Options section.

As you move into the Paste Options section of this shortcut menu Word will display the copied text in the document to let you see the result of each paste option. The copy is only completed after you choose the icon in the Paste Options dialog box.

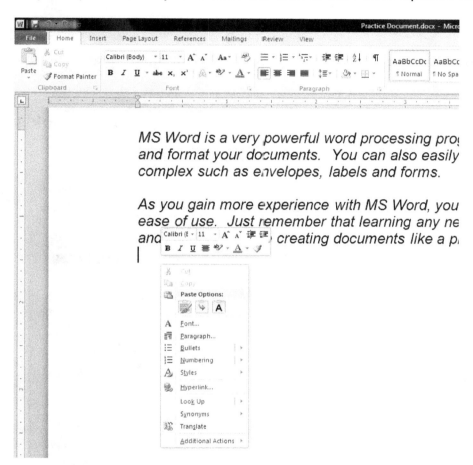

You have now copied the first paragraph using shortcut menus.

6.   Move to the beginning of the copied paragraph with (Control+Up Arrow) and insert a blank line above it by pressing (Enter).

Using Drag and Drop to Move and Copy

In addition to the Cut and Paste method, you can also drag selected text to move or copy. However, this method works best when the source and destination are on the same screen.

In other words, the drag and drop method does not work well when you are trying to move or copy text from one page to another because scrolling through a multiple page document is not very accurate. Aside from being inefficient, this practice can lead to confusion and messed up documents.

To move or copy using the drag and drop method, you first select the text you want to move or copy. Then, move the mouse pointer into this text. Next, press and hold the **RIGHT** mouse button and drag to the destination. When you release the mouse button, you will see a shortcut menu asking you to select Move or Copy. You could have also held the left mouse button down as you were dragging, but then the end result would have been moving the text. You will not see the option to copy unless you drag with the right mouse button held down.

1. **Select the second paragraph in this document (click three times).**

2. **Move the mouse pointer into this paragraph and press and hold the Right mouse button.**

3. **Keeping the RIGHT mouse button held down, move the mouse pointer to the bottom of this document and release the mouse button.**

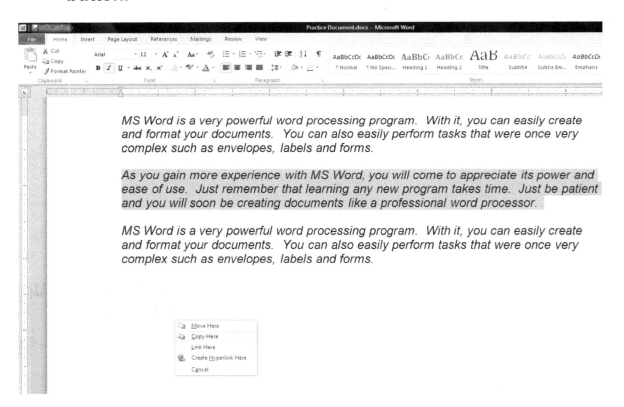

4. **Choose Copy Here from the shortcut menu to create a duplicate of the second paragraph and place it at the bottom of this document.**

© 2011 Luther M. Maddy III

5. Press the (Down) arrow to deselect the paragraph.

After moving or copying, it is very important to deselect the text. If you do not and begin typing, the text you just moved, or enhanced, will be replaced with the new text. Deselecting simply removes the blue highlighting and returns the text to the normal editing mode.

6. If needed, add a blank line above the paragraph you just copied by pressing (Enter) at the beginning of that paragraph.

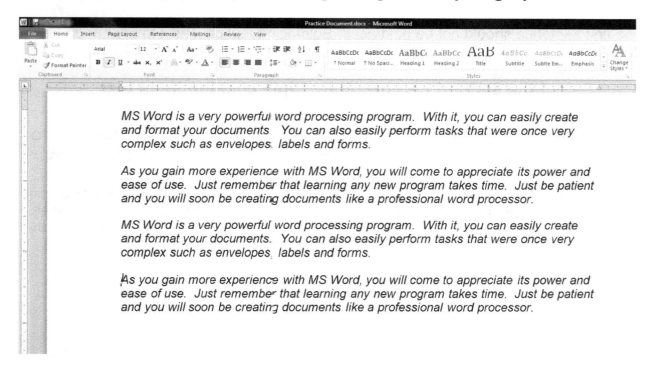

You document should now appear like the above.

Enhancing Existing Text

To change the appearance of text that is already created (existing text), you must first select the portion of the text you wish to change. After selecting the text, you then apply the formatting options you want, such as Bold, Italic or other Font attributes.

1. Press and hold (Control) and click anywhere in the first sentence of the first paragraph.

   (Control+click) selects an entire sentence.

2. With this sentence selected, click the Bold tool on the Ribbon.

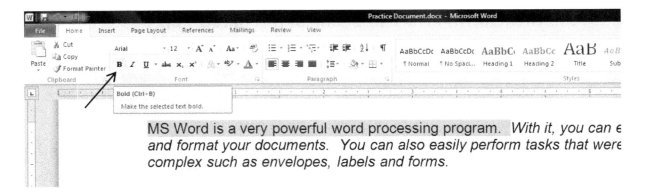

The first sentence should not be boldfaced. Boldfacing text causes it to appear darker than the text around it. If you cannot see the Bold tool, click the Home tab.

3.   Select the second paragraph by triple clicking in its text.

4.   In the Font group, click the Font dialog box launcher (the   to the right of Font) on the Ribbon to display the Font dialog box.

In this portion of the lesson you are using the Font dialog box to change the appearance of the text. You could also use the tools on the ribbon to change these options as well. The Font dialog box however, allows you select some options that do not appear on the ribbon.

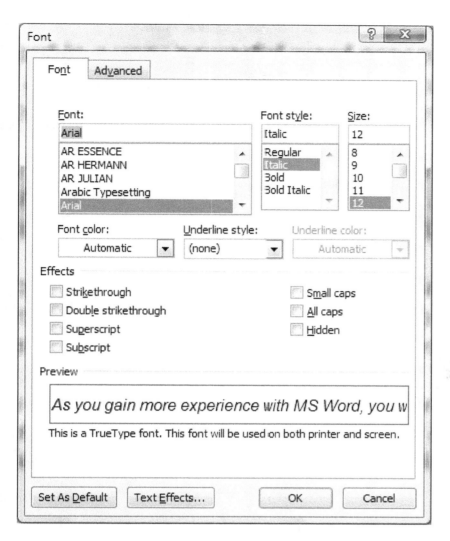

5.   In the Font dialog box, choose Arial from the font selections.

Scroll down this list of font faces if needed.

The Preview section will show you how selected text will appear with the options selected in the Font dialog box.

6.   Click in the Size section of this dialog box and select a font size of 24.

7.   Click the Font Color drop down list button. From the list of colors, choose Blue then click OK.

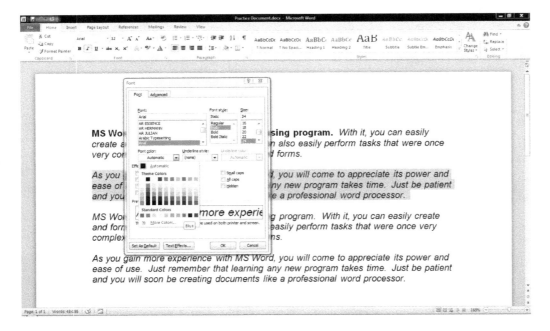

Clicking the More Colors option in the color selection area allows you to choose many more colors than the standard colors listed on the main color selector.

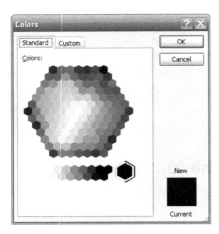

You can try the more colors option on your own as you are experimenting with Word. The best way to learn a software program is through experimenting on your own. This book is guiding you through some options, but you should not hesitate to practice the things you are learning here on your own.

8.   Deselect this paragraph by pressing (DOWN arrow).

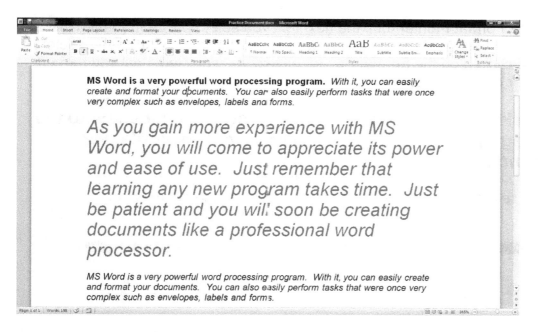

The second paragraph should now have the font options you selected. If Word changed the entire document, click the Undo tool on the quick access toolbar to have just the second paragraph change.

Using the Format Painter

If you want another portion of text to be formatted the same as some other text in your document, you do not have to repeat all the formatting commands you used originally. Instead, you can use the Format Painter. The Format Painter will copy formatting from one portion of text and allow you to use that formatting on additional text. The Format Painter is accessed from the Clipboard ribbon on the Home tab.

You'll now see how the Format painter command works.

1. **Move the insertion point anywhere in the text that is formatted with the Blue, Large font and click the Format Painter tool on the Home tab.**

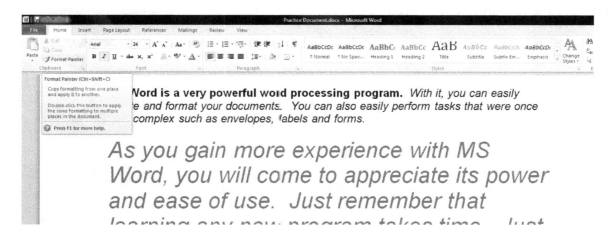

Once you click the Format Painter tool, the next text you select will be formatted just as the text was where you clicked this tool. Word will format only the next text you select. If you had double-clicked on the Format Painter all text you selected, until you turn off the Format Painter option, will be reformatted.

2. **After clicking the Format Painter tool, move the mouse into the first paragraph and select the two consecutive words, *your documents.***

The text you just selected should be formatted the same as the entire second paragraph.

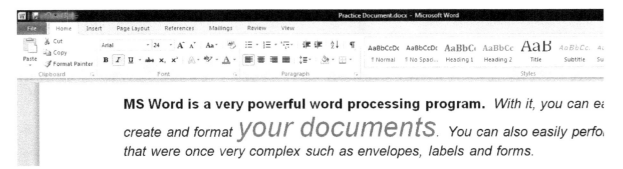

If more text is formatted than you expected, click the Undo tool on the Quick Access toolbar and that should correct this.

Using the Mini-Toolbar to Enhance Text.

As you've already seen, there are several methods available for you to enhance text. Now you're about to learn one more, using the mini-toolbar. When you select text the mini-toolbar is available in the background just above the selected text. You can activate the mini-toolbar by moving into it. In this portion of the lesson you'll use the mini-toolbar to bold and underline a word.

1. **In the first line of the first paragraph, select the word *easily.***

You should now see the mini-toolbar in the background just above the selected word.

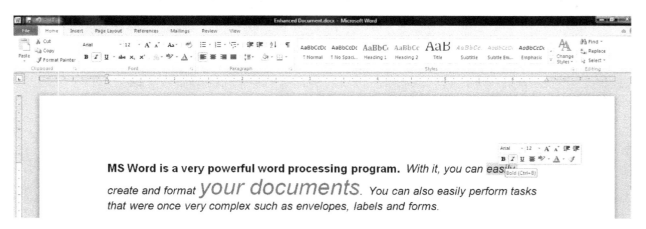

2.   Click the Bold and Underline tools on the mini-toolbar.

The word *easily* should now be boldfaced and underlined.

Using Keyboard Shortcuts to Enhance Text.

Ok, so now your head is probably spinning with so many ways to enhance text. But, before you give up in frustration, let's show you one more method, not to confuse you but to show you, again, that there are a variety of ways to perform most commands. Keyboard shortcuts give us a very quick way to perform commands when our hands are on the keyboard.

So, to give you an idea of how this works, we'll have you select and underline a word using only the keyboard.

1.   Move to the beginning of the document with (Control+Home).

The insertion point should now be at the beginning of this document.

2.   Hold the shift key down and hit the (Down) arrow twice.

The first two lines of this document should be selected. Holding down the Shift key selects text when you move using the keyboard.

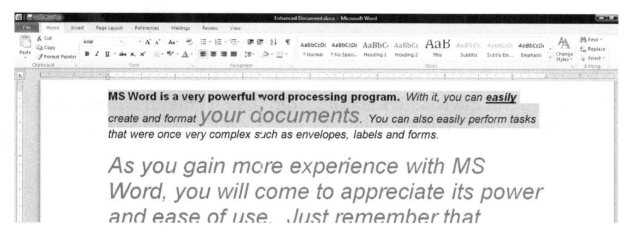

3.   With these two lines selected, press (Control+U).

Control+U is the keyboard shortcut for underlining.

4.   Press (Down) again to de-select this text.

Are you confused yet?

Let's take a break and let the spinning in your head slow down. You've just seen several ways to do the same thing. This was not done to confuse you, but to simply make you aware that there are a variety of ways to perform some commands.

When there are several methods available, there is no one right way. The way that you can remember is the right way. There is no reason to try to memorize every possible way to do every command in Word. Instead, learn the method that appeals the most to you and get very comfortable with that method. Then, as you become more comfortable with Word in general, you can increase your productivity by learning additional, perhaps faster ways to perform the commands you use the most.

Using Save As instead of Save

When you use the Save command, the document changes are saved under the original name. This lets you add to the document as you make changes or add text.

Sometimes, you may wish to keep the original as it was and also save the changes. In this case, you would use the Save As command to make a new document (file) from the document on your screen. The original stays as it was as long as you did not use the Save command after making changes.

In this portion of the exercise you will create a new document from the changed version of the document you are currently working with. The original will remain as it was before you started making these changes.

1. **Choose the Save As command from the File menu and name this file as:** *Enhanced document.*

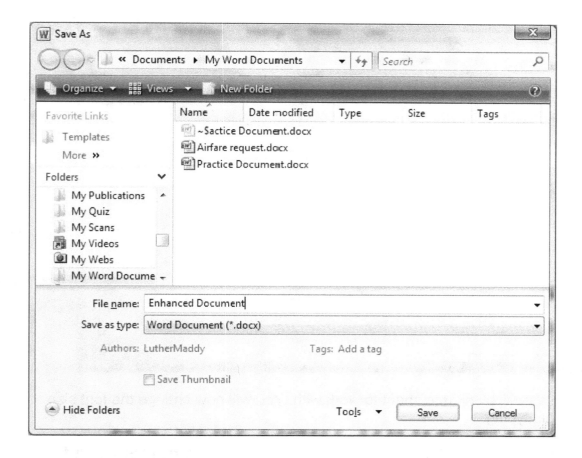

2.   Choose Close in the Office Button menu to close this document.

Enhancing New Text

So far in this lesson you have only changed or enhanced existing text. To do this you had to select the text you wanted to change and then tell Word how to change that text. Only the text you selected changed.

In this portion of the exercise, you will create a new document, formatting and enhancing it as you create it. To have the next text appear with an enhancement, you will turn on the feature you want then type the text. When you do not want that formatting option anymore, turn it off. Once you turn on an enhancement, it will stay on until you turn if off.

1.   Choose the New command in the File menu and click Create to create a new Blank document.

You now have a new, blank document to work with. You will now change the font size before you begin typing.

## 2.	Use the Font Size tool on the Ribbon to change the font to 14 points.

This time you are using the tools on the Ribbon to change font attributes rather than the Font dialog box as you did previously. Neither of these methods is superior but, depending on which options you intend to use, the individual tools are probably faster than turning on the dialog box and then making the changes.

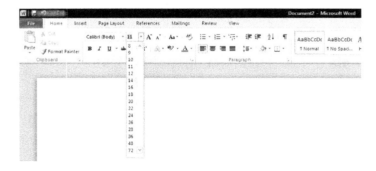

As you click the drop down list button on this tool you can select from many pre-set font sizes, the larger the number the larger the font. One point is approximately $1/72^{nd}$ of an inch; therefore 72 points would mean the letters would be 1 inch tall.

3. **Click the Center tool in the Paragraph group to change the alignment to Center.**

You should notice that the insertion point moved to the center of the text area. Word will automatically center what you type next. This centered text will be the heading of a memo you are going to create.

4. **Type *Memorandum* and press (Enter) twice.**

Centering remains on. To return to left aligned text you will have to turn off centering by selecting the left align tool.

5. **After typing this line, click the Align Left tool in the Paragraph group to change the alignment back to Left.**

6. **Change the Font Size back to 12 points.**

We only want the centered heading to be larger than the rest of the text so you are changing the size back to the commonly used 12 point size.

Now you're going to create the text of the memo. This text uses Boldfacing, Underlining and Strikethrough enhancements. As you create this text you will "turn on" an enhancement when you want to use it and "turn off" the enhancement when done. You can find Bold and Underline tools on the ribbon. However, to use the strikethrough enhancement you will have to display the Font dialog box.

7. **Now, use the Bold, Italic, Strikethrough, and Underline options from the Ribbon and the Font dialog box launched from the font group to create the following text:**

To: *John Smith*
From: *Susan Johnson*
Date: *February 22, 2012*
Subject: *Word Classes*

Using a word processor is actually <u>fun!</u>

*Not too long ago, I didn't even know what a ~~word processor~~ was. Actually it's **very easy** to use. I just had to learn a few of the basics and then **<u>everything</u>** began to make sense.*

*Since I can now **prove** that I can do this, I expect everyone else to learn too. From now on, Word classes will be mandatory for all staff.*

You should type the above text even though it is not shaded here. We purposely left off the shading this time so you could see the other enhancements.

> **Hint:** Some formatting options work like toggle switches. When you are finished using an enhancement such as Bold facing, click the same tool to turn off the feature!

8. **When done, save this document as *Memorandum*, then close the document.**

Removing Enhancements

To remove enhancements such as Bold, Italic and Font Changes, begin by selecting the text you want unenhanced. Then, with the text selected, turn off the options you do not want. If you want to remove all of one type of enhancement, such as boldfacing throughout an entire document, you can select the entire document and then "turn off" boldfacing. This is what you will do in the next portion of this exercise.

1. **Open the *Memorandum* document**

2.   Select the entire document with (Control+A).

You've just used a keyboard shortcut to select the entire document. With a large document this would be much more efficient than trying to use the mouse to click and drag through the entire document.

3.   Click <u>twice</u> on the Bold, Underline and Italic tools on the ribbon.

You have now removed all the Bold, Italic, and Underlining from this document. You click each of the tools twice because the first time, Word applied that option to the entire document. The second time, it removed that option from the entire document.

4.   Save and close the *Memorandum* document.

The Clear Formatting Option

MS Word also has a clear formatting option that you can use to quickly remove all formatting. To use this option:

1. Open *Enhanced Document*, then click the Styles dialog box launcher (the [x] to the right of Styles) to display the styles drop down list.

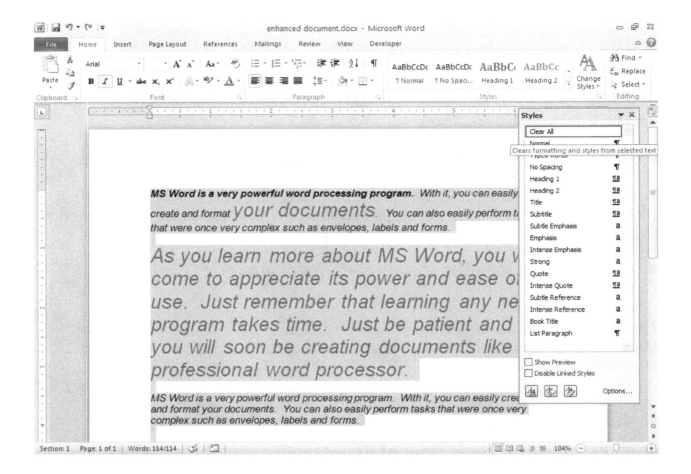

3. Select the entire document with Control+A, then select Clear All in the styles list.

At this point, all formatting from the selected text will be removed.

* Note: you can also select the clear formatting option from the Styles drop down list in the Styles group on the Home ribbon.

4.   Close the Change Styles list.

5.   Save and close the document.

Skill Builder Lesson #4

1.   **Open Airfares Request.**

2.   **Move to the top of the document. Create two new blank lines at the top. Then, move back to the top, center, change the font to 14 points and type:**

     No Fault Travel Agency
     143 San Andreas Fault Line
     Hollister, CA 93992

3.   **Use the Copy and Paste commands to copy the company name, "No Fault Travel Agency" below the booking agent's name.**

Try using Paste Options to match destination formatting. Otherwise, you can to change the alignment back to left and the font back to 12 points yourself.

4.   **Enhance the company name at the top of the letter with: Arial, 24 point, Blue text.**

Your document should now appear like that below.

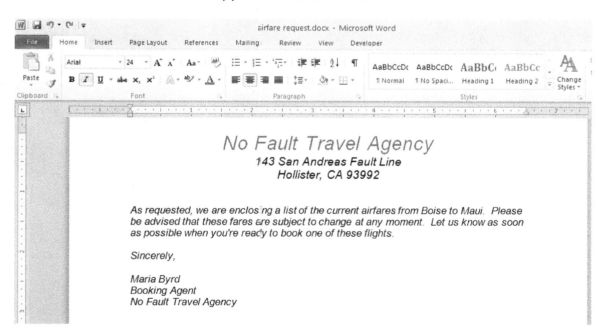

5.   **Save and close this file.**

Check Yourself

Questions:

1. Describe two ways to select a paragraph.
2. List two methods for copying text.
3. Using the keyboard, how do you move to the end of the document?
4. Identify two methods for bolding text.
5. How do you deselect text?
6. What is the purpose of the format painter?
7. What dialog box do you use to find other formatting tools for fonts?

Lesson #5: Basic Paragraph and Page Formatting

In this lesson you will learn to:

Change Document Margins
Change Line Spacing
Create Hanging Indents
Indent Paragraphs
Use Tab Stops

Lesson #5: Basic Paragraph and Page Formatting

In the previous lesson you changed the appearance of the text (words) within the document. In this lesson you will focus on changing the layout of the document. Changing the layout will include options like the top, bottom, left and right margins and features like line spacing and paragraph indentation. In addition to these features this lesson will also have you explore tab setting, which is a feature that lets you quickly put information in single spaced columns.

Page Setup

In MS Word, many formatting options are available in the Page Setup tab. Here you can change document margins, paper size, orientation and other document options. In this exercise you'll select a few of these options to become familiar with their use.

1.   Use the File menu to create a New Blank Document.

You can also use the keyboard shortcut of (Control+N) to create a new document. There is no reason to memorize the entire list of keyboard shortcuts. However, as you become more confortable with Word you will find that you can become more productive by learning a few shortcuts for the commands you often use.

2.   Right+Click the Status bar and turn on Vertical Page Position if it is not already on. Click in the text area to close this menu when done.

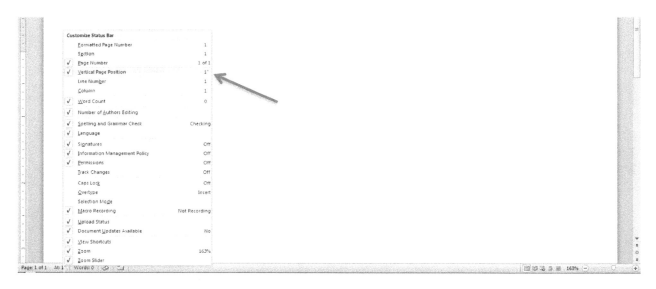

When you examine the status bar now you should see *At: 1"*. This shows you that the insertion point is 1" below the top edge of the printed paper. This represents the current top margin setting.

© 2011 Luther M. Maddy III

You're now going to change the margins for this document. Creating a smaller top margin will allow text to appear closer to the top of the printed page. The next document you create will include a letterhead which usually appears closer to the top edge of the page than 1" down.

In cases where you are using preprinted letterhead, you will likely want to make the top margin larger. Otherwise the text you type may appear in the letterhead instead of below it. To find out what your margin settings should be, grab a ruler and measure from the top edge of the page to the place below the letterhead you want your text to begin.

3.   Click the Page Layout tab on the Ribbon.

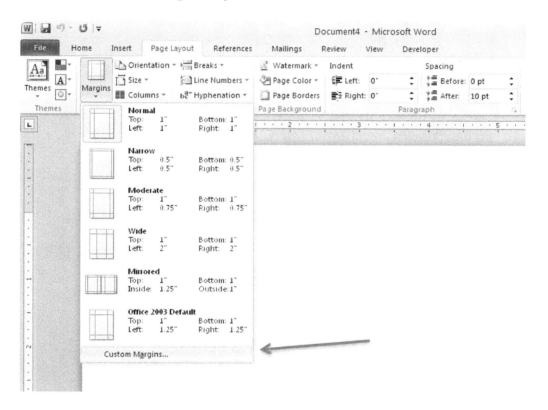

4.   Click the Margins tool and choose Custom Margins.
While there are many pre-set margin options you can choose from, the Custom Margins dialog box lets you set exactly the margins you want. In "real" use of Word, you can easily change margins by selecting one of the pre-set margin settings.

By default, Word's margins are 1" on the top and bottom and 1." in the left and right. You can change these settings for a variety of reasons.

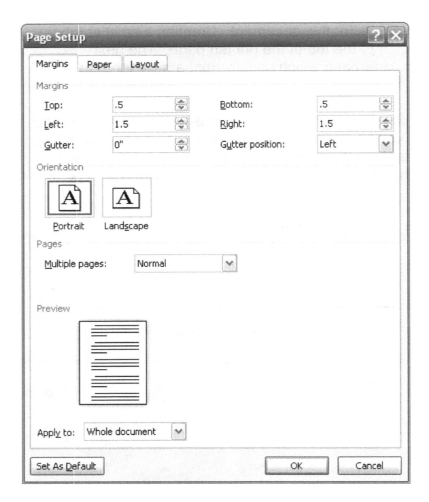

5. Type .5 to Change the Top margin to .5 in.

Press (Tab) to move from field to field within this dialog box. When you are in the correct field, just type the value you want.

6. Change the Left and Right margins to 1.5" each.

7. When done, click OK.

Since you are in Print layout view, you will see the margin changes reflected on both ruler bars. If the horizontal ruler is not visible in the Print Layout view, click the View tab and turn on the Ruler option on the ribbon. After making this change, the Status bar should also show that the vertical position of the insertion point is at .5", reflecting the new margin setting.

8.   **Click the Home tab and change the alignment to Center (use the Center tool on the Ribbon) and type:**

   No Fault Travel Agency
   143 San Andreas Fault Line
   Hollister, CA 93992

9.   **Change the alignment back to Left and then press (Enter) twice.**

Pressing (Enter) twice creates two blank lines between the letterhead and the text you are about to create.

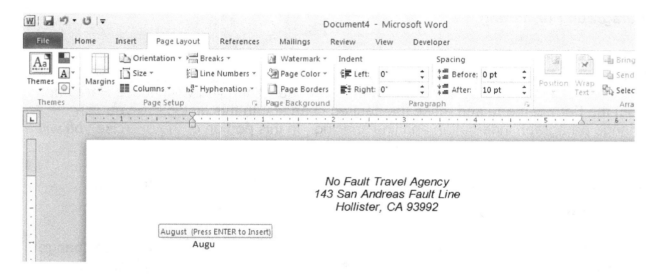

10. **Begin typing the name of the current month such as _August_. If you see a box displaying the month's name above the letters you just typed, press (Enter).**

This is the AutoComplete feature. It will only work for months that have more than five letters. Word will complete often repeated words for you.

11. **After the month is complete, press (Space). If you see the AutoComplete box with the current date displayed above the text you are typing, press (Enter) to insert the entire date.**

12. **Press (Enter) twice to accept this date and move one line down the page.**

13.   Two lines below the date, type the following:

Mr. and Mrs. Martin Johnson
343 Overland Dr.
Boise, ID 83709

Dear Mr. and Mrs. Johnson,

14.   Create two new blank lines below the salutation by pressing (Enter).

Paragraph Formatting

To change the appearance of text you have not typed yet, you simply select the formatting options you want and then type the text. To change existing paragraphs, you'll first select the paragraphs you want to change. Then you will choose Paragraph from the Format menu and make the desired changes. In this dialog box you can change paragraph indentation and line spacing. In this portion of the exercise you will change paragraph formatting for new and existing test.

1.   Open the Paragraph dialog box by clicking the dialog box launcher (   ) to the right of Paragraph on the Ribbon.

You should now see the Paragraph dialog box. You will use this dialog box to change the line spacing to double. You could have also used the Line Spacing tool on the Ribbon. This dialog box allows you to change many additional settings.

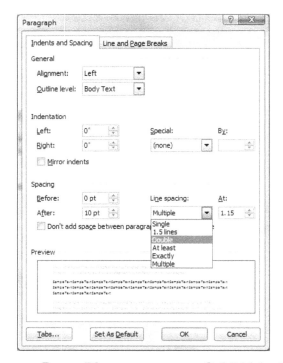

2.   **In the Paragraph dialog box, click the Line spacing drop down list button and choose Double as the line spacing.**

Spacing Between Paragraphs

You have been adding blank lines between paragraphs by pressing the (Enter) key. Word has the ability to do this for you automatically. It does this with the Paragraph Spacing option. If you examine the Paragraph dialog box you'll see the Spacing section here. You should also notice there is a setting for Before and After a paragraph. By default (automatically) Word inserts 10 points after each paragraph. This is helpful and eliminates you having to press (Enter) between each paragraph. However, while you're learning Word, we're going to have you change this setting to 0 points so that each blank line only occurs when you press enter.

3.   **In the Paragraph spacing section, ensure that both the Before and After are set to 0.**

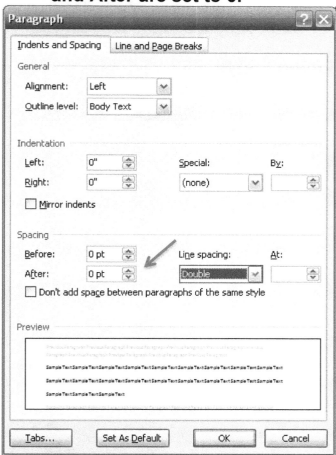

You should also notice the *Set As Default* button at the bottom of the Paragraph dialog box. If you click this button, any changes you have made here will be applied automatically when you create a new document. We won't have you do this until you learn a little more about Word and the options you want to make automatic.

4. Click OK to close the Paragraph dialog box.

From this point on, all text you type will be double spaced until you change this setting back to Single. And, if you thought this was the only way to change line spacing you should know better by now. You can also change the line spacing very easily on the Ribbon on the Paragraph group of the Home tab and you'll use that method as well later.

5. Type the following paragraph, and press (Enter) when done:

We just wanted to let you know that your trip to Bangkok, Thailand is coming together nicely. We have scheduled several trips and tours that will enable you to see much of this beautiful country. In the following paragraphs you'll find some important information about your trip.

This paragraph should be double spaced. Now, you will use another method to change the line spacing back to single.

6. Click the Line Spacing tool on the Ribbon and change the line spacing back to Single.

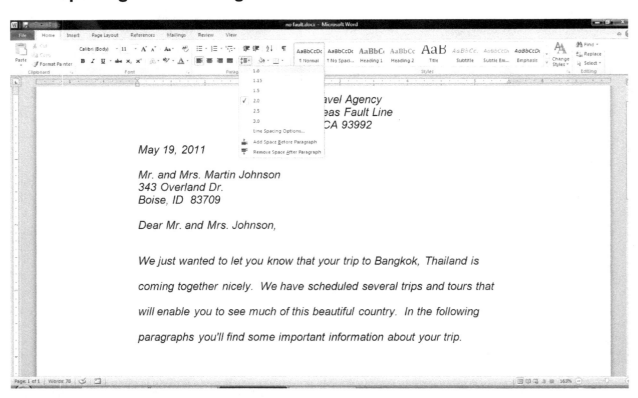

Indenting Paragraphs

If you wish to offset one or more paragraphs from the text around it you can indent that text. The Indent command will cause the entire paragraph to move to the right, rather than just the first line.

7. Use the Ribbon and change the Font Size to 8 points.

8. Locate and click the Increase Indent tool on the Ribbon one time to indent the next paragraph.

Each time you click the Increase Indent tool it indents .5" to the right. If you wanted to indent this paragraph 1", you would click this tool twice.

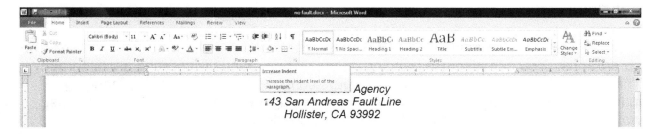

9. Then, type the following paragraph and press (Enter) when done:

Remember that any problems you have on your trip will not be our fault. We will not be held responsible for any loss of life, limb or luggage. You assume all risks yourself.

Notice that the entire paragraph is indented.

10. Change the Font size back to 12 points and press (Enter) twice.

Just like many other commands that affect the appearance of text, the Indent command stays "on" until you turn it off. If you do not change the indent level back to the original setting, all additional text will be indented.

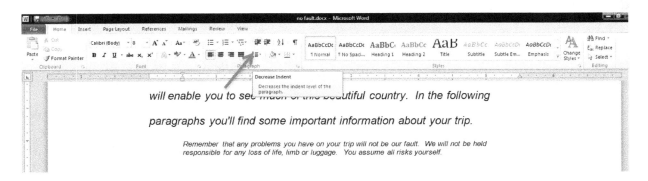

will enable you to see much of this beautiful country. In the following

paragraphs you'll find some important information about your trip.

Remember that any problems you have on your trip will not be our fault. We will not be held responsible for any loss of life, limb or luggage. You assume all risks yourself.

11. Click the Decrease Indent tool to end paragraph indentation.

You will find the Decrease Indent tool just to the left of the Increase Indent tool. This tool also decreases the indent in increments of .5" each time you click it.

12. Turn on Underlining and type: *Your Itinerary:* then press (Enter) twice.

13. Turn off Underlining before continuing.

This is the only text you want underlined. Remember changes, once turned on, stay on until you turn them off.

Hanging Indents

Word has different indenting styles. Hanging indents are useful for bulleted or numbered paragraphs. You can also use hanging indents when manually creating a bibliography. There is no default tool for the hanging indent command. You can create hanging indents from the Paragraph dialog box or even using the ruler. However, the easiest way to turn this feature on is with the keyboard shortcut (Control+T).

1. Press (Control+T) twice.

Like the other indent command, the hanging indent uses increments of .5". Each time you pressed Control+T the left indent marker on the ruler moved .5".

2. Now, type *5/1/15* and press (Tab).

When you press (Tab) the insertion point will move to the bottom indent mark. All lines within the paragraph you are typing will now indent to this mark.

3. **Type the following paragraph and notice that it "hangs" off the date.**

Arrive in Bangkok at 11:45 p.m. Next you'll travel to your hotel and check in. After checking in you will begin your tour of the countryside.

4. **Type the following two paragraphs by typing the date first, then pressing (Tab ➜) before typing the text. Use the (Enter) key to insert blank lines between these paragraphs.**

5/2/15   Recover from jetlag. Do nothing.

5/3/15   Leave Bangkok and return home.

You should notice you did not need to re-do the hanging indent command for each hanging paragraph. Once you turned this feature "on", it stays until you turn it "off".

5. **Press (Control+Shift+T) twice, or until you see the paragraph indent marks both return to the Left margin on the horizontal ruler.**

This turns "off" the hanging indent feature.

6. **Now press (Enter) twice and type the following text:**

Thank you for choosing No Fault Travel. Please call if you have any questions.

Cynthia Anderson
Booking Agent

Your document should now appear similar to the one below:

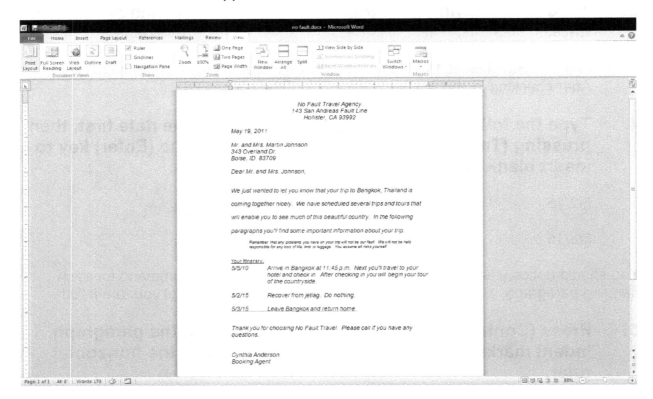

7.   Save this file as *Johnson Confirmation Letter* and close it.

Setting Tabs

Tab setting is very easy in Word. You use tabs to place portions of your text in single spaced columns. Anytime you want to put text in columns, you should consider setting tabs. You can use the Ruler bar if you only need basic tab settings. If you want to add dots or other leaders between the tabular columns, you can use the Tabs dialog box from the Format menu.

Setting tabs eliminates pressing the (Space) bar numerous times after completing the text in one column and moving to the next column, which is extremely more productive. When you set a tab stop, you move the next column with only one keystroke, the Tab key. Setting tabs also ensures the columns will be perfectly aligned.

Word allows several different types of tabs to be set, depending on the alignment you would like in the columns.

1.   Use the File menu to create a New Blank Document.

2.   Click the Center tool on the Ribbon and type:

Table of Contents

3.   Press (Enter) to move down the page and change the alignment back to Left.

Using the Ruler to Set Tabs

To set tabs on the Ruler, you simply click where you want the tab to appear. You do not need to worry about deleting the existing tab stops, which occur every .5". Word automatically erases the default tab stops as soon as you place your own tab on the Ruler.

You can also set right, center, and decimally aligned tabs using the Ruler. To do this, select the tab type you want by clicking the Tab button at the very left edge of the horizontal ruler. Word allows you to set; Left, Right, Center and Decimal tabs. Each tab type controls how the information in the tabbed column will be aligned.

1.   Point, but do not click on the tab button at the far left edge of the Ruler. (Make sure the Tab is set to "Left" – see graphic)

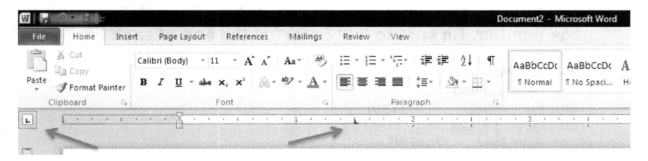

You should notice the tool tip informing you that this button represents a left tab. If it says something other than left, click this button until the symbol changes to appear as an "L", representing a Left Tab.

2.   Now, carefully click at the 1.5" mark on the horizontal Ruler.

You have now set a tab stop at this location. This is verified with the "L" mark on the ruler at this position. If you do not set the tab exactly where it should be, you can move it by carefully dragging it to the correct location.

If you attempt to move a tab marker, make sure you click precisely on the tab. If not, you may find that you have set an additional, incorrectly placed tab. In this case you can click on the extra tab and drag it down, off the ruler to remove it. You are setting a

Left tab, not because it is on the left of the page, but because you want the columned information to be left aligned at the tab stop.

3.   Move the mouse pointer back to the tab selector button at the left edge of the Ruler bar.

4.   Click on this button twice, then move the mouse away from this button and then back to the button. You should now see that you have selected a Right Tab.

5.   After selecting the Right tab, click at 4.75" on the Ruler bar to set a right tab there.

You selected a Right tab because the information in this column is to be right aligned at the tab stop.

6.   Now, type the following, pressing (Tab➜) before each topic and page number. Be sure to hit "Enter" at the end of each line.

```
(Tab)  Getting Started    (Tab) 1
(Tab)  Basic Editing      (Tab) 5
(Tab)  Formatting         (Tab) 10
(Tab)  Moving & Copying   (Tab) 22
(Tab)  Auto Text      (Tab) 30
```

Your document should now appear like the illustration below.

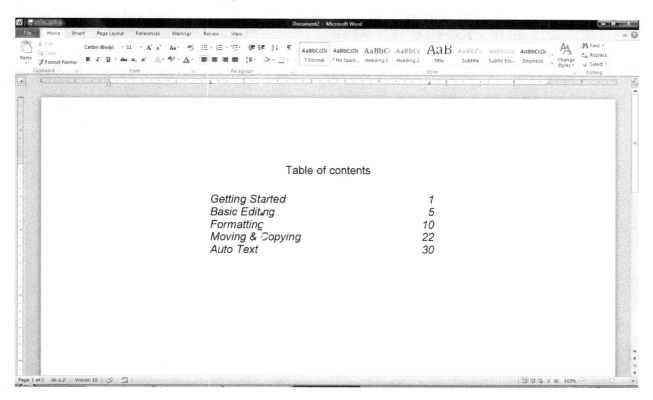

Using Tab Leaders

Word allows you to select a variety of leaders between tabbed columns. You can choose from dots, dashes or solid lines. To set leaders, you can enter the Tabs dialog box from the Paragraph dialog box. To add leaders to existing text, as you will do here, you will need to select the text you want to change first.

1. **Use the keyboard to move to the beginning of "Getting Started" in the tabbed information.**

Be careful not to select the blank line above or below the tabbed information.

2. **Press and hold the Shift key. Then move to the end of the last page number with the (Down) arrow.**

You have used the keyboard to select this text for accuracy.

3.	**Launch the Paragraph dialog box (click** 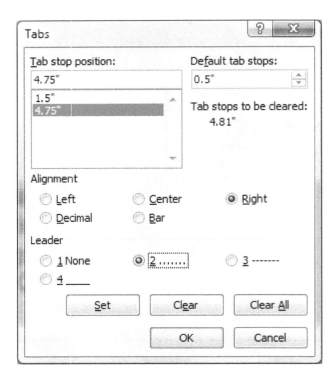 **) and click the Tabs button at the bottom left of this dialog box.**

4.	**In the Tabs dialog box, click on 4.75" in the Tab stop positions section of this dialog box.**

If you did not set your tab exactly at 4.75", it will not matter. Simply select the second tab in the list. If you have more than two tabs set here, you can click on the one you do not want and click the Clear button to remove it.

5.	**Next, click Leader option #2.**

You have chosen to place dots between the columns. If you are making more than one change you would need to click Set after each change. This is not necessary this time because you have made only one change.

6.	**Click OK when done.**

You should now see leaders between the columns you just created.

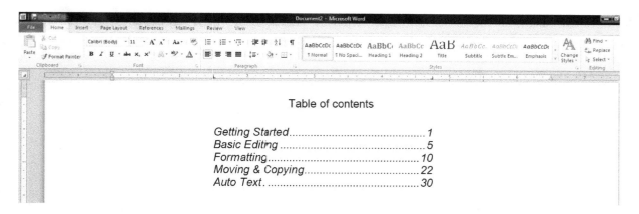

Adjusting Tabs with the Ruler Bar

To move a tab, just drag it to the desired location on the Ruler bar. Of course, it you want the change to affect existing text, make sure you select the text before you make the change. To remove a Tab, drag it off the ruler bar and into the document window.

1. **Move to the end of the document. Make sure you are below the last line in the tabbed columns.**

2. **Carefully click the tab marker at 1.5" and drag it into the text to remove it. Do the same with the tab at 4.75".**

3. **With the insertion point two lines below the last line in the tabbed columns, click the Increase Indent tool on the Ribbon once. Next type:**

    The Increase Indent tool makes it very easy to indent single paragraphs. When you are creating new text, the indent command stays on until you turn it off.

4. **Press (Enter) after this paragraph. Click the Decrease Indent tool in the Paragraph group. Next, type the following paragraph:**

    When you no longer want your paragraphs indented, click the Decrease Indent tool.

Your document should appear similar to the one below. Again, your lines may break differently depending on the font you are using.

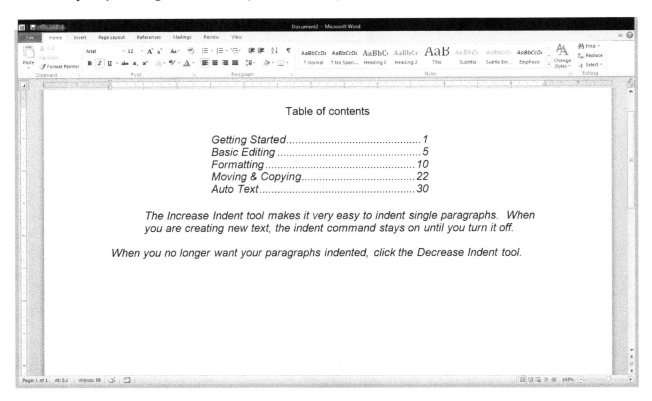

5. **When done, Save this file as *Tab Practice* and Close it.**

1. **Open Airfares Request.**

2. **Change the Top Margin to .5".**

3. **Move to a line above the letter closing. Make sure you have at least 1 free line (press Enter) between the paragraphs and the closing line.**

4. **Next, set a left tab at 1.5" and a decimal tab at 4.75" on the ruler bar. After setting these tabs, type the following using the appropriate Tabs ➔:**

   ➔   SouthWest   ➔   225.00
   ➔   United ➔   444.00
   ➔   Delta   ➔   1019.00
   ➔   Value Jet   ➔   89.00

5. **After creating the airfare list, add dot leaders between the columns.   (Hint: Paragraph to Tabs)**

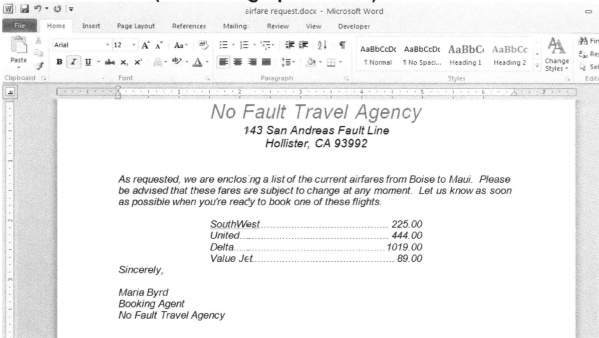

6. **Save and close the file.**

Check Yourself

Questions:

1. What tab do you find the tools to change your margins?
2. What is the default margin setting for MS Word?
3. When might you use the AutoComplete function?
4. How do you change the line spacing from single to double?
5. What happens when you press (Control+T)?
6. How do you set the tabs on the ruler?

Lesson #6: Envelopes & Labels

In this lesson you will learn to:

Create Envelopes and Labels from Letters
Create an Entire Sheet of Labels

Lesson #6: Envelopes and Labels

It is very easy to create either envelopes or labels from letters you have written. In this exercise, you'll open a previously created letter and create an envelope to mail that letter. After creating the envelope, you'll create an entire sheet of labels with *No Fault Travel's* return address.

Creating Envelopes

To create an envelope, first write the letter. Then, open the mailings tab and select labels in the Create Group. Word will then automatically pull the mailing address from the letter and place it on the envelope.

1.   Open *Johnson Confirmation Letter.*

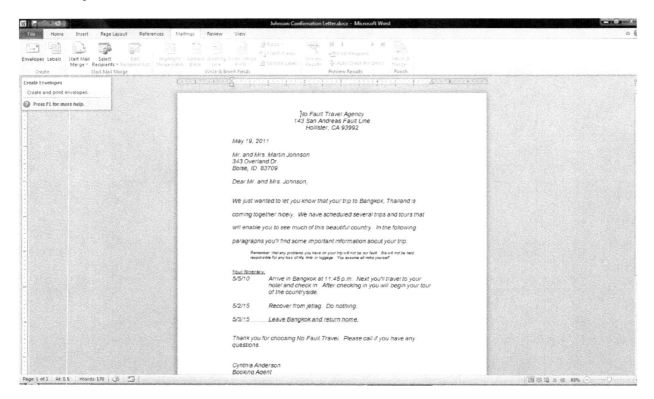

2.   Choose the Envelopes tool from the Mailings tab.

You should now see the Envelopes and Labels dialog box.

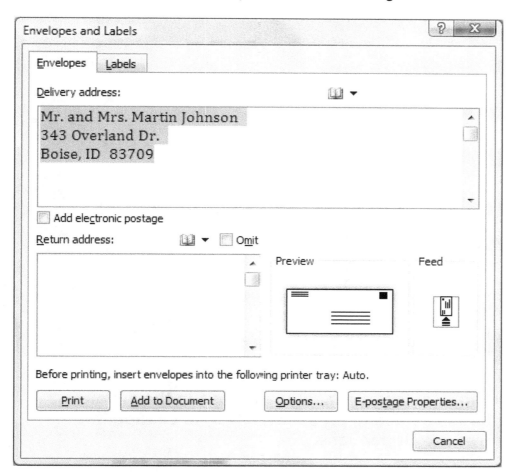

Word automatically copies the mailing address for this letter into the Envelopes and Labels dialog box. Rather than printing, you'll add the envelope to your letter so you can change the case of the address. After adding it to the document, you could also change fonts, add graphic images and add other enhancements to the envelope.

3.   If needed, click the Envelopes tab, then click Add to Document.

You should now see that Word has added the envelope to the top of the letter. You will now place the address in all Uppercase with (Shift+F3), the shortcut for this. Uppercase meets current US Post Office requirements for bulk mailing discounts.

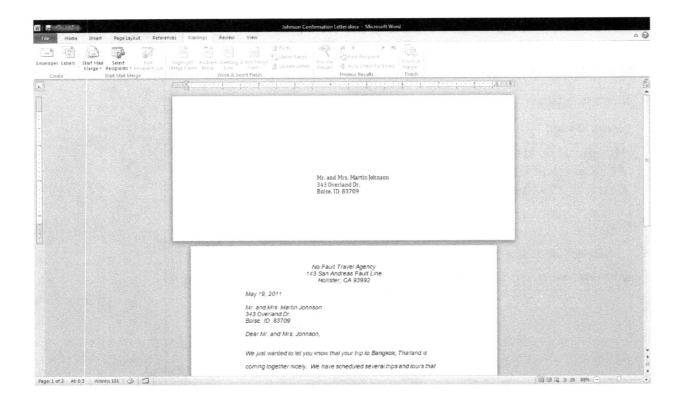

4.   **Click and drag to select the mailing address in the envelope. With the address selected, press (Shift+F3) to change the mailing address to Upper case.**

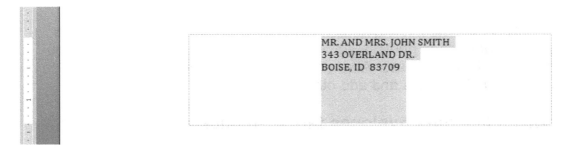

Any punctuation in the address in the letter will be duplicated on the envelope. If you are receiving bulk mailing discounts, you will want to remove the commas and other punctuation. If you do not want to remove punctuation each time you create an envelope, you may consider omitting the punctuation in the address when you type it in the letter.

Creating Labels

You'll now create an entire sheet of labels with No Fault Travel's return address. You can also create one label for the mailing address. If you prefer to print labels instead of envelopes, you can tell Word which label to start printing on. This lets you run label sheets through the printer more than once. However, if you do this, use extreme caution and examine the label sheet for loose labels before you do. You may find, as in this example, that printing an entire sheet of the same label is practical even for mailing addresses if you use them repeatedly.

1.   Move to the top of the letter with (Control+Pagedown). Select the return address at the top (No Fault Travel).

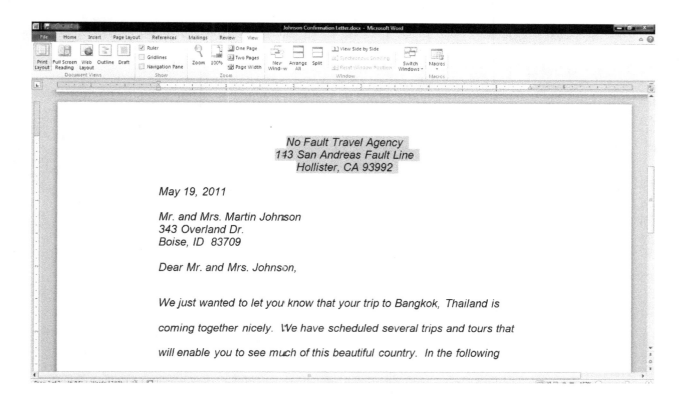

2.   After selecting the return address, click the Labels tool in the Mailings tab.

You should now see the labels dialog box. The next step will be to tell Word what kind of labels you are using and whether you want one label or an entire sheet of the same label.

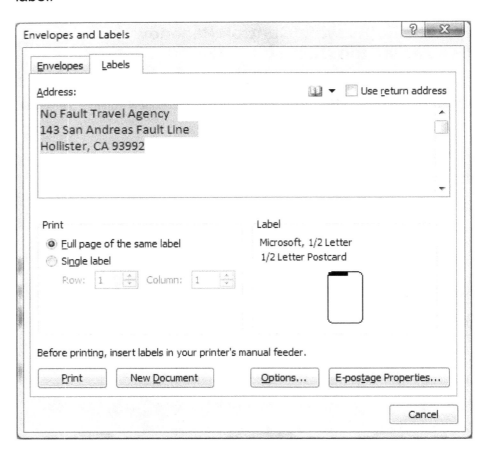

3. Click the Options button.

You will now need to tell Word what brand of label you are using and that vendor's label number.

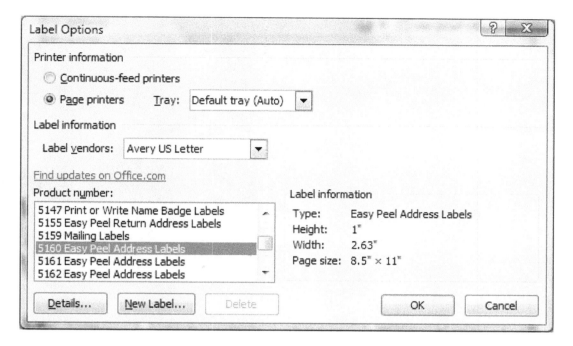

4. **Click the Label vendors drop down box and select Avery US Letter as the vendor. Next, scroll down to and select 5160 in the Product number section.**

5. **After choosing the label type and size, click OK.**

You have now returned to the labels dialog box. Now you need to tell Word if you want to print just one label or an entire sheet of the same label. Since we are printing labels for the company name, we'll select an entire sheet of the same label.

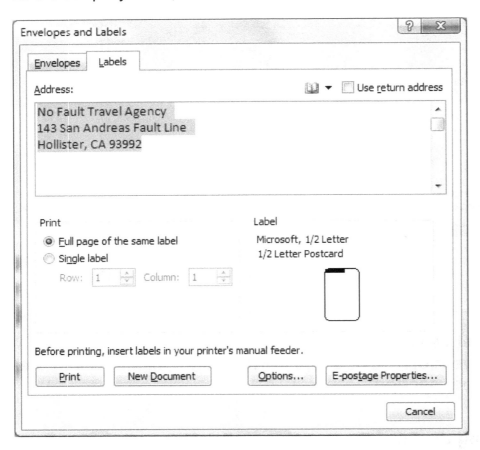

6. **Ensure the Full page of the same label radio button is selected and then click New Document.**

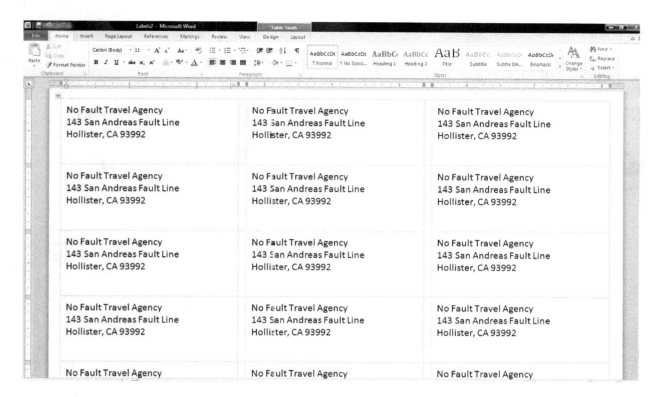

You should now see that Word has created an entire sheet filled with the return address of No Fault Travel. You'll now select the entire sheet of labels and change the font to make it consistent throughout.

8. **Save the labels as *No Fault Return Addresses* and close both files saving changes.**

Skill Builder: Lesson #6

1. Open *Airfare Request*

2. Add an envelope to the document with the following address:

Because this document has no inside address you'll have to type the above address as you are creating the envelope. If you had Betty's address in the letter, Word would automatically insert it into the envelope.

3. Save and close *Airfare Request.*

Check Yourself

Questions:

1. What tab do you find Envelopes and Labels on?
2. What label size is Word currently set to use?

Lesson #7: Find, Replace and Thesaurus

In this lesson, you will learn to:

Find and Replace Text
Find Synonyms

Lesson #7: Find and Replace

Finding Text

The find command does what its name implies. It finds text. You can use it as a "go to" command to find a particular heading or phrase quickly in your document.

Replacing Text

The replace command finds text and lets you change it to something else. This command is useful when you have, for example, consistently misspelled a name throughout the document.

When you use the Replace command you have the option of replacing every occurrence of the text automatically or selecting which ones you want to change and which you do not.

In this exercise you will use the replace command to change the travel agency's name from No Fault Travel to Faultless Travel.

1.   Open the file named *Johnson Confirmation letter*.
The first page of this document is now the envelope you created in the last lesson. You will now move down to the second page, the beginning of the letter itself to being the Find operation.

2.   Move to the top of page 2 by pressing (Control+Page Down).

3.   Click the Home tab and then click the Replace tool (far right) on the Ribbon.

4.   **In the Find what section of this dialog box type *No Fault Travel* and press (Tab).**

5.   ***In the Replace with section of this dialog box, type *Faultless Travel*.***

After specifying what to find, and what you want to change it to, you then must decide how you want to accomplish the replace. Clicking Replace All will replace every occurrence of No Fault with Faultless.

If you are not sure you want to change every single occurrence, then you would click Find Next. After finding the next time No Fault Travel occurred in the document you could then replace that one instance with the Replace command. If you did not want to replace that instance, you would click Find Next to find the next time that text appears in the document.

6.   **Click Replace All.**

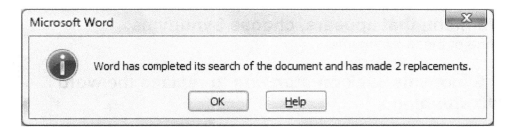

7.   **Click OK when Word informs you how many replacements it made. After this, close the Find and Replace dialog box.**

You have now effectively changed the name of this company with one command. Scroll through the document to verify that this change has taken place.

Using the Thesaurus

The Thesaurus allows you to find synonyms for words you have used in your document. To use the Thesaurus, move the insertion point into the word for which you want to find synonym. Then, display the Review tab and choose Thesaurus in the Proofing group. You can also quickly display synonyms by right clicking the word.

The Thesaurus will then display synonyms for that word. You then have the option of replacing that word with one of the listed synonyms, or you can lookup synonyms for any of the suggestions.

7.   Move the insertion point into the word *beautiful* and Right+Click.

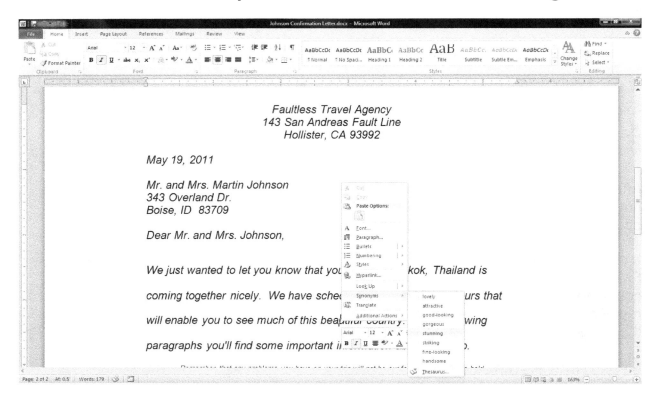

8.   From the sub-menu that appears, choose Synonyms.
You will now choose one of these synonyms.

9.   In the list of Synonyms click on *stunning* to replace the word beautiful with stunning.

10.   Save and close this document.

1. **Open *Airfare Request.***

2. **Use the Replace command to change all occurrences of *Maui* to *Hong Kong***

3. **Replace all occurrences of *Value Jet* with *Alaska Airlines*.**

4. **Find a suitable synonym for the word *list* in this document.**

5. **Save and close the file.**

Check Yourself

Questions:

1. What two options do you have with the replace command?
2. Where do you find the Thesaurus?

Lesson #8: Creating and Formatting Tables

Word tables are very versatile. You can use them to draw attention to a portion of your document. Or, you can use tables as an easy way to put information in columns. You can even use tables to perform basic math operations. In this exercise you will create and then format a table. You will also insert some totaling cells.

1.   **In a New Document, click the Table tool on the Insert tab. Then, click and drag down and right to create a table of 5 columns and 6 rows.**

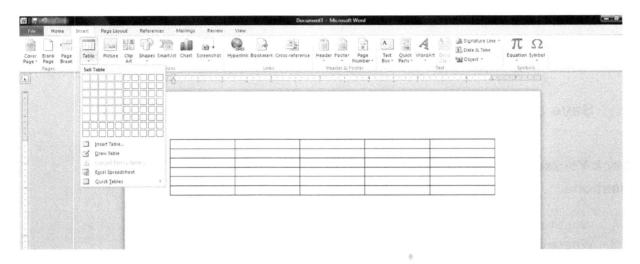

Merging cells

When you create a table, every cell (the intersection of a row and column) is of equal size. You will now merge all the cells in row one to create one large cell for the table's title.

1.   **Select all the cells in row 1 of the table you just created.**

You can select all these cells by clicking and dragging across them or by clicking in the selection area (left margin) just to the left of the first column.

2.   **After selecting these cells, right+click in the selected cells. From the shortcut menu, choose Merge Cells.**

© 2011 Luther M. Maddy III

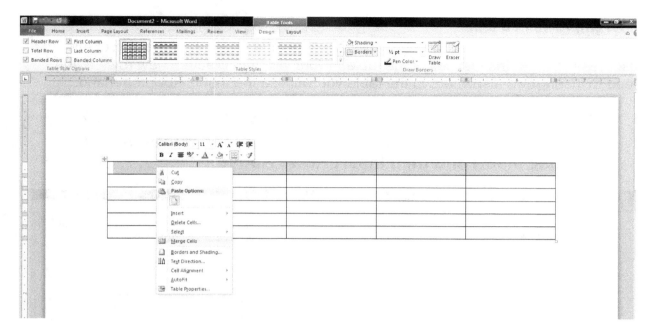

The separation lines between the cells in the first row should disappear. All the cells in row one have merged into one, larger cell.

3.   In the first cell in this table, click the Center tool on the Home tab and type:

# of bookings by location

4.   Press (Tab) to move into the next table cell.

The Tab key moves one cell forward each time you press it. Shift+Tab will move one cell backward.

# of bookings by location				
	Jan	Feb	Mar	Apr
Maui	22	56	65	34
Kauai	45	34	43	121
Oahu	43	99	66	23
Total				

5.   Fill in the table as shown in the figure above. Use (Tab) to move forward and (Shift+Tab) to move back cell by cell.

Inserting rows in a table

You can easily insert new rows in a table. If you need a new row at the end of the table, just press (Tab) in the last cell of the table. Word will then create a new row. If you need to insert rows elsewhere in the table you will use the Insert Row command.

1.   Move into the selection area just to the left of the first row (outside the table) and right+click. From the shortcut menu, choose Insert and then Insert Rows Above.

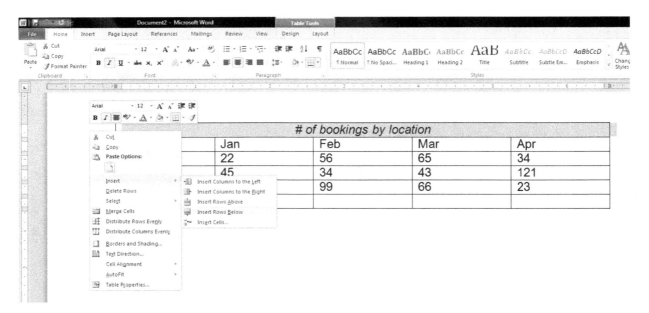

Word has now inserted a new row above the first row. Here you will enter an additional title.

2.   Move into the new row at the top of the table and type:

No Fault Travel Hawaii Destinations

You don't need to turn centering on because Word copied the structure (merged cells) and formatting of the cell you selected to insert this new table row.

Splitting Table Cells

If you need to, you can split a cell or cells into more than one cell. You can do this by choosing the Split Cell command from the Table menu. You can also do it with the Draw Table tool. In this portion of the exercise, you will use the Draw Table tool.

1. **Click the Design tab. Then, click the Draw Table tool.**

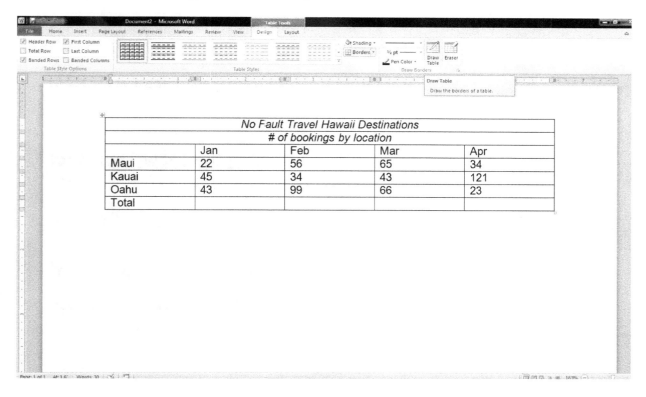

The draw table tool provides a very quick way to split several cells as you are about to do.

2. **Use the Draw Table tool and draw a line to the right of the names, beginning in the cell above Maui as shown in the figure below.**

© 2011 Luther M. Maddy III

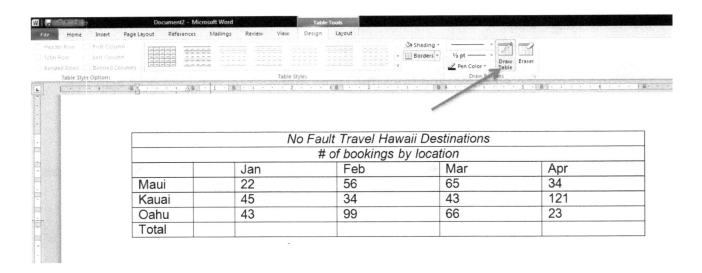

3. **Turn off the Draw Table mode by clicking the Draw Table tool again.**

If you don't turn off the draw table tool, Word will attempt to create table cells wherever you click.

4. **Select all the cells in the new column you just created.**

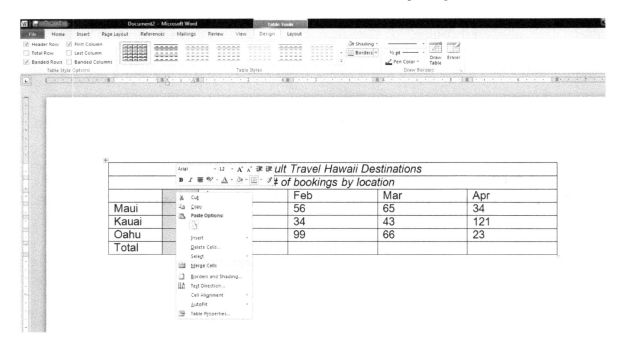

5. **Right+click in the selected cells and chose Merge Cells from the shortcut menu.**

7. **In this newly merged cell type:** *Island*

Changing Text Direction

The text may not fit well in this cell. You could increase the size of this column to make the text fit. However, you will instead rotate the text to make it fit in the cell. You can change the text direction in a cell easily using the Text Direction tool on the Layout tab.

1. **Staying in the cell where you just typed** *Island,* **display the Layout tab and then click the Change Text direction tool.**

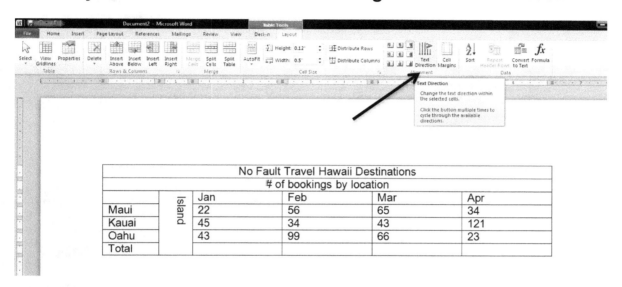

The text in this cell now goes down instead of across in the cell.

2. **Now, click the Center tool on the Home tab.**

The text is now centered vertically in the cell.

Table Cell Alignment

If you examine the cell that contains the word *Island*, you should notice the text is not perfectly aligned in the cell. You have centered the text horizontally, which appears to be centered vertically because of the change in the text direction. Now, you will change the vertical alignment of this cell. And, because of the change in text direction, the change will appear as a horizontal change rather than vertical. However, this should all make sense after you complete the command.

1.   Right+Click in the cell containing the word *Island* and choose Table Properties from the shortcut menu.

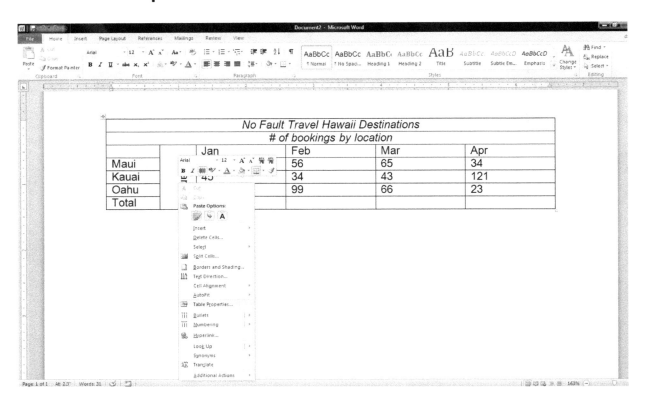

You should now see the table properties dialog box. Here you can change many attributes of the table, rows, columns or individual cells. For now, we'll use this to change the vertical alignment of this cell.

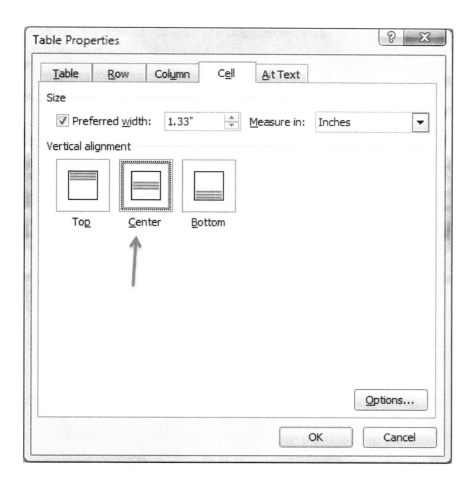

2.   **In the Table Properties dialog box, click Cell to display Cell properties. Then, click Center in the Vertical alignment section and click OK.**

You should now notice that the text in this cell is centered both horizontally and vertically.

Formatting the Table

You can easily add formatting options to tables. In this portion of the exercise you will change cell alignment, shade rows and rotate text.

1.   **Select all the cells that have numbers in them. Also, select the row that will have totals too.**

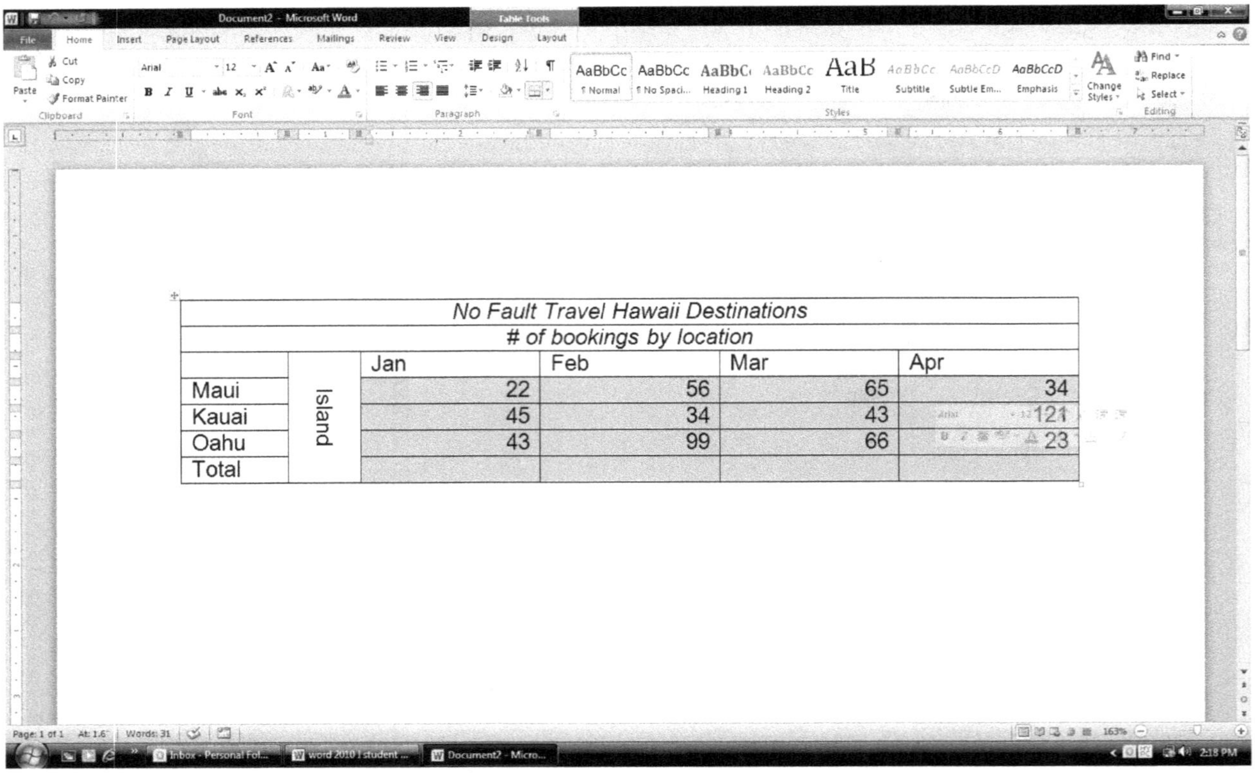
Document2 - Microsoft Word
Table Tools
No Fault Travel Hawaii Destinations
# of bookings by location
Jan
Feb
Mar
Apr
Maui
Kauai
Oahu
Total
Island
22
56
65
34
45
34
43
121
43
99
66
23

2. With these cells selected, change the alignment to right, with (Control+R).

Of course, you could use another way to change the alignment, such as the Ribbon, and achieve the same results.

Table Formulas

You can use the Formula option in the Table Layout tab to add formulas to table cells..

1. Click the Layout tab then move into the cell that will display January's total.

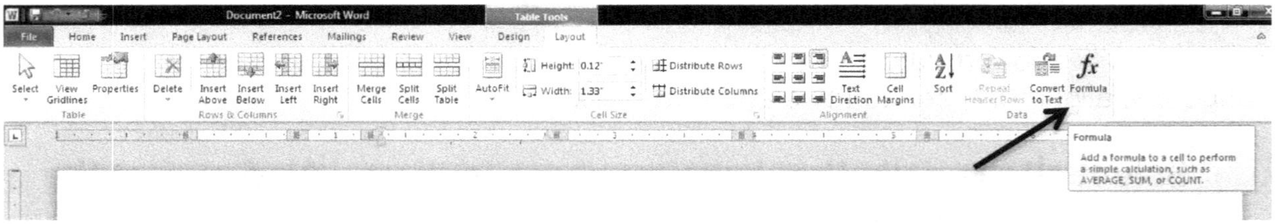
Document2 - Microsoft Word
Table Tools
Formula
Add a formula to a cell to perform a simple calculation, such as AVERAGE, SUM, or COUNT.

2. Click the Formula tool on the Layout tab.

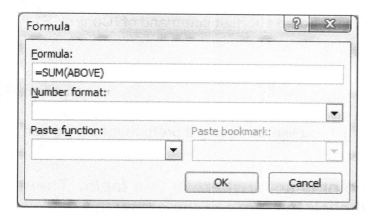

You should now see the Formula d alog box. Here you can enter a formula to do basic math within a table cell.

3.   Make sure the formula reads *=Sum(Above)* in the formula text box, then click OK.

This formula tells Word to add up a l the numbers above it.

4.   Move to the bottom of the next column and click Formula and then OK to enter a formula there.

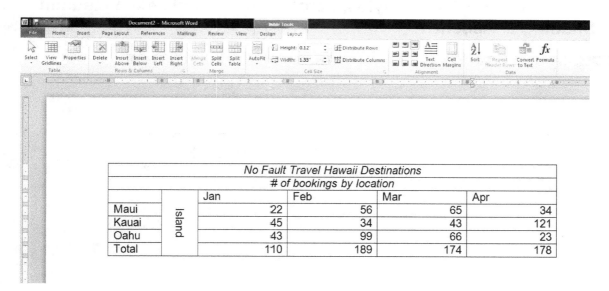

No Fault Travel Hawaii Destinations					
# of bookings by location					
		Jan	Feb	Mar	Apr
Maui	Island	22	56	65	34
Kauai		45	34	43	121
Oahu		43	99	66	23
Total		110	189	174	178

5.   Repeat this process for the remaining totals.

6.   Select the cells with the month names and then click the Center tool on the Home tab.

Not to confuse you, but if you had use the keyboard shortcut command of (Control+E), you would have saved a step.

Using the Table Styles

Word provides many preformatted Table styles to choose from. You can always manually change the borders and shading if you like, but using a preformatted style can be much faster.

1.   Ensure that the insertion point is somewhere in this table. Then, display the Design tab and click the More down arrow in the Table styles section.

2.   From the list of Table Styles, scroll down to and select Medium Shading 2, Accent 1.

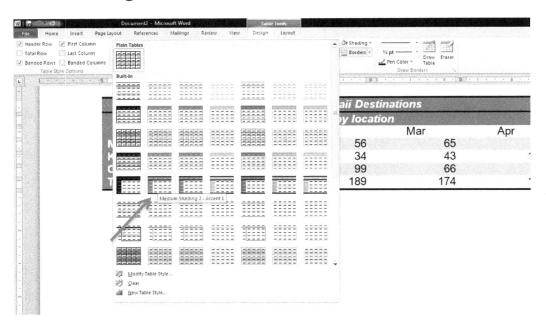

If you apply a table style and later change your mind, you can apply any other style from this list. When you do, the existing style is completely erased and the new style takes over.

3.   **After examining the appearance of the table, display the list of Table Styles again.**

4.   **This time choose Colorful Grid Accent 5 in the last row of styles.**

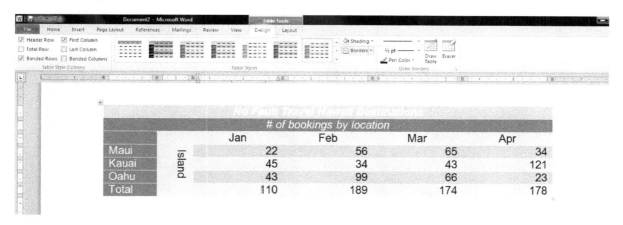

Notice that the new style took over completely. Table styles, however, will not overwrite formatting that you have done yourself. For example, the month names remain centered regardless of the table style you choose.

Changing Column Widths

If you examine this table closely you may notice that the columns do not need to be as wide as they are. In fact, making the width of the columns with the numbers smaller would probably enhance the appearance of this table. There are, of course, several ways to change the width of a column within a table, but for this exercise we'll have you use the Auto Fit method.

5.   **Right+Click in any table cell and choose Auto Fit from the Shortcut menu.**

6. Next, choose AutoFit to contents.

You should notice that the table is much smaller as Word adjusted each column to fit the width of the text within it.

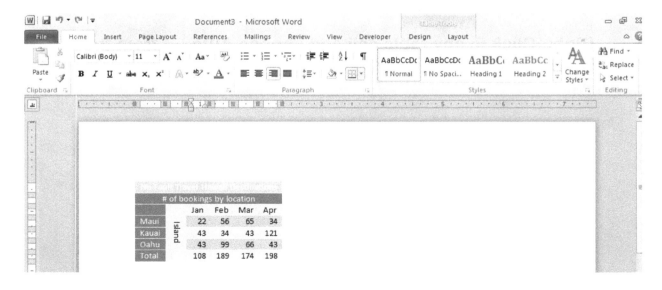

Now you'll center the table on the page by using the Table Properties dialog box.

© 2011 Luther M. Maddy III

7. **Right+Click in the table and choose Table Properties from the shortcut menu.**

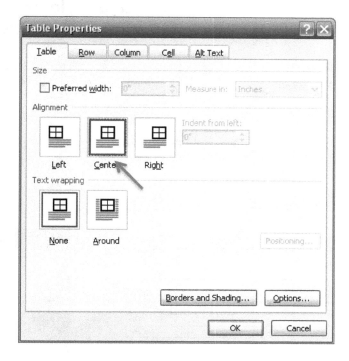

8. **Click the Table tab to ensure the Table properties are showing then click the Center tool in the Alignment Section.**

You are telling Word that you want the table to be in the center of the page rather than aligned with the left margin.

9. **Click OK when done.**

10. **Save this as *Hawaii Destinations* and close it.**

Skill Builder: Lesson #7

1.   Open *Airfare Request.*

2.   Delete the list of airlines and prices and replace it with a table as shown.

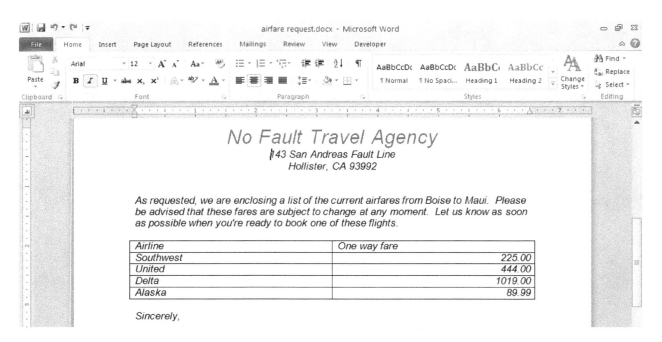

3.   Use the table properties dialog box to change the column widths and center the table so it appears as the one below:

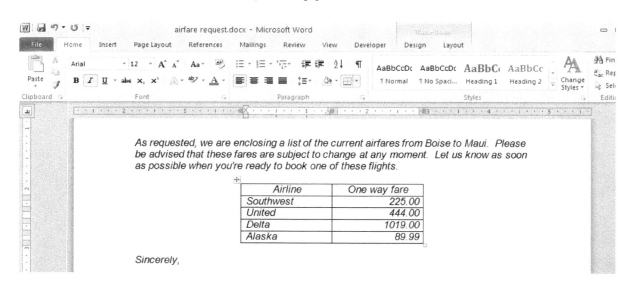

4.   Apply an attractive table formatting style and then Save and Close this file.

Microsoft Word Shortcut Keys

<u>Feature</u>	<u>Shortcut key</u>
Align Center	(Control + E)
Align Justify	(Control + J)
Align Left	(Control + L)
Align Right	(Control + R)
Close a file	(Control + W)
Copy text or graphics	(Control + C)
Cut selected text to the clipboard	(Control +X)
Font	(Control +D)
Increase Indent	(Control + M)
Italic	(Control + I)
Margin Release (hanging indent)	(Control + T)
Page Break	(Control + Enter)
Paste the clipboard contents	(Control + V)
Print	(Control + P)
Redo	(Control + Y)
Replace	(Control + H)
Save	(Control + S)
Underline	(Control + U)
Undo	(Control + Z)

Index

Adjusting Tabs 69
Auto Text..................................... 66
Draft View.................................... 9
Drag and Drop.............................. 35
Enhancing 37
Envelopes 74
   Creating 74
Finding Text 84
Hanging Indents 62
Help... 26
Indenting 61
Labels.. 74
   Creating 76
Moving and copying 31
Moving the Insertion Point............... 19
Opening Files 18
Page Setup 54
Paragraph Formatting 58
Print Layout View 9
Print Preview 11, 13
Printing 12
Replacing Text 84

Ribbon..................................... 2
Ruler 3
Save vs. Save As 7
Saving 4
Selecting Text 30
Shortcut Keys............................... 103
Spell check.................................. 21
Splitting table cells......................... 91
Status Bar 2, 3
Tab Leaders 67
Table Autoformat...................... 98, 99
Tables 88
   Changing text direction 93
   Formatting 95
   Inserting rows 90
   Merging cells 88
   Splitting table cells 91
Tabs 64
Title Bar................................. 2
Undo.. 33
Views..................................... 9

Other books that may interest you

Down But Not Out: Hope and Help for the Unemployed
This book provides encouragement and practical advice for those dealing with a career transition of any kind, but especially unemployment. This book includes steps to maintain a positive attitude, resume tips, and advice on making the best interview impression possible. Online training and workbook also available.

Retail price: $12.95

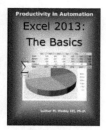
Excel: The Basics (2013 or 2010)
In "learning by doing" you will gain a good grasp of the basics of Excel. You'll learn to create formulas, format and print worksheets, copy and move cell data, and generate attractive charts and graphs from your Excel data.

2013: Retail price: $9.95   2010: Retail price: $8.95

Excel: Beyond The Basics (2013 or 2010)
In "learning by doing" you will gain a good grasp of the Excel features beyond the basic level. You'll learn to create advanced formulas using Excel functions like PMT(), IF(), VLookup() and more. You'll also learn about worksheet protection, data validation, creating and using templates, advanced charting features, and much more.

Retail price: $9.95

Excel: Database and Statistical Features (2013 or 2010)
In "learning by doing" you will gain a good grasp of the Excel database features. You'll learn to create and use Pivot Tables and Charts. You'll also learn about database functions like DSum() and DAverage(). You'll also learn about filtering and subtotaling Excel data. Finally, you'll learn about performing statistical analysis using the Analysis Toolpak.

Retail price: $9.95

Word: The Basics (2013 or 2010)
In "learning by doing" you will learn the basics of MS Word. You'll also be introduced to performing tasks the most efficient way possible to increase your productivity. This workbook covers document creation and editing. You'll learn to copy and move and enhance text. You'll also learn about page a paragraph formatting, setting tabs, creating tables and more.

2013: Retail price: $9.95   2010: Retail price: $7.95

Word: Enhancing Documents (2013 or 2010)
In "learning by doing" you will learn the some of the desktop publishing features of Word. You'll learn to place text in columns, use Autoshapes, enhance mailing labels, and use and create styles. You'll also learn to add hyperlinks to your documents, how to use pre-defined templates, and much more.

2013: Retail price: $9.95   2010: Retail price: $8.95

Order wherever books are sold. Ordering in quantity?
Save 20% by ordering on our website: **www.LutherMaddy.com**